Rural Sanitation in India

About the Editors

Kumar Alok is an Indian Administrative Service (IAS) officer of the 1990 batch and presently working as Joint Secretary at Ministry of Home Affairs, Government of India. An M. Tech from Indian Institute of Technology (IIT), Kanpur, in Aeronautical Engineering, he is a social development professional with wide-ranging experience in various social sectors. He has long and rich experience in sanitation and hygiene promotion at the national level in India as well as in an international agency—UNICEF. He played a key role in designing and scaling up of India's national rural sanitation programme while working as Director, Rural sanitation in the Department of Drinking Water Supply in the Ministry of Rural Development, Government of India. He was responsible for initiating a large number of innovations in 'Total Sanitation Campaign (TSC)'- the flagship rural sanitation programme in India, including designing and operationalizing the innovative incentive scheme, Nirmal Gram Puraskar and an effective online monitoring system for TSC. These innovations were instrumental in revamping and rejuvenating the rural sanitation programme in India. He has authored a book "Squatting with Dignity: Lessons from India" which presents a detailed account of the development of the rural sanitation movement in India in the last decade and has been published by SAGE Publications in January 2010.

Dr. A.P. Singh is currently working as Associate Professor at National Centre for Good Governance (*Erstwhile* National Institute of Administrative Research), Kosy Nook, Lal Bahadur Shastri National Academy of Administration, Mussoorie. He has acquired wide – ranging experience while working as an academician as well as a researcher for almost all social sectors. He also worked as a Consultant in UNICEF and was posted at Ministry of Drinking Water and Sanitation, Government of India for one year. He has several published works in journals of repute and books to his credit and has been associated with successful completion and publishing of several research studies of different social sectors for rural areas.

Rural Sanitation in India

Compendium of Case Studies

Edited by

Kumar Alok

A.P. Singh

Published for

National Centre for Good Governance

Lal Bahadur Shastri National Academy of Administration, Mussoorie-248179

by

CONCEPT PUBLISHING COMPANY PVT. LTD.

NEW DELHI-110059

ISBN-13: 978-81-8069-925-2

First Published 2014

Published and Printed by

Since 1974

Concept Publishing Company Pvt. Ltd.
A/15-16, Commercial Block, Mohan Garden
New Delhi-110059 (India)
T: 25351460, 25351794, *F*: 091-11-25357109
E: publishing@conceptpub.com, W: www.conceptpub.com
Editorial Office: H-13, Bali Nagar, New Delhi-110 015, India.

Cataloging in Publication Data--*Courtesy:* D.K. Agencies (P) Ltd. <docinfo@dkagencies.com>

Rural sanitation in India : compendium of case studies / edited by Kumar Alok, A.P. Singh.
p. cm.
Includes bibliographical references and index.
ISBN 9788180699252

1. Sanitation, Rural--India--Case studies. 2. School hygiene--India--Case studies. 3. School health services--India--Case studies. I. Kumar Alok, 1965- II. Singh, A. P.

DDC 363.72091734 23

niar

National Institute of Administrative Research

Renamed as
National Centre for Good Governance

Fostering Excellence in Governance

Kush Verma, IAS
Director General

Lal Bahadur Shastri National Academy of Administration Mussoorie

Foreword

A recent newspaper article in a National daily gave Indians a wake-up call by stating that the country possessed more mobile phones than toilets. This is borne out by a look at the national statistics (Census 2011) which reveal that nearly 70 per cent of the rural population has no toilet at home. Further analysis reflects that about 92.40 per cent of homes in rural Jharkhand, 86.90 per cent in Madhya Pradesh and 85.90 per cent in Bihar have no toilet. It is distressing to note that reports of manual scavenging still surface from a few pockets in the country and that the topic was the subject of a powerful presentation in an episode of Aamir Khan's 'Satyamev Jayate'.

It is a fact that 1/3rd of 2.5 billion people worldwide without improved sanitation live in India. It is also true that the majority of those practicing open defecation live in rural areas. Open defecation in rural areas is prevalent extensively in the developing world. In the Indian context, it is applicable even to those who are comparatively well off or are above the poverty level. It clearly indicates that open defecation is a major behavioural concern for India.

However, it is encouraging to note that four out of ten people who have gained access to improved sanitation since 1990 live in India and China (WHO). A closer look reveals that the momentum for better sanitation practices is building up in all States. It is felt that the best practices of the leading States need to be documented and shared with the States that have been left behind in the implementation of the Total Sanitation campaign. This cross learning can help us in

Cozy Nook Complex, Charleville Road, Mussoorie - 248 179 (Uttarakhand) INDIA
Office: +91-135-2632485 Fax: +91-135-2632686 EPABX: +91-135-2632663, 2630917 Ext.: 210
Website: www.lbsnaa.ernet.in

enhancing the coverage of rural sanitation. Experiences from best practices in the sanitation sector demonstrate that sanitation projects are not successful without the involvement of the community. It is important that the community should own the responsibility of the project. Many successful practices have been implemented in different parts of India for improving Sanitation coverage.

Keeping the above in view, it was felt necessary to document the best practices in sanitation promotion from various districts of India. This book tries to capture thirteen case studies from different parts of the country covering various aspects of the sanitation programme so that the District and State officials are able to draw lessons and improve the programme implementation in their respective areas. The case studies have been written by practitioners of rural sanitation i.e. the District and State Officials and NGOs directly involved in the programme implementation. They have tried to discuss the key issues and strategies to overcome challenges citing actual examples. The book highlights key learning elements from these case studies which can be used by others in the sanitation sector as well as in other social development programmes.

I would like to gratefully acknowledge three years of academic hard work and efforts put in by the editors of the volume Shri Kumar Alok, IAS and Dr. A.P. Singh in documenting the Case Studies. I would also like to place on record my appreciation of the support provided by UNICEF in bringing out this volume.

18th June 2014 **Kush Verma, IAS**

Contents

Abbreviations

ANM	-	Auxiliary Nurse Midwifes
APHL	-	Additional Primary Health Centre
APL	-	Above Poverty Line
ASHA	-	Auxiliary Social Health Activist
ATM	-	Automated Teller Machine
AWC	-	Anganwadi Centre
BDO	-	Block Development Officer
BEP	-	Bihar Education Project
BPL	-	Below Poverty Line
CBO	-	Community Based Organisation
CCDU	-	Communication and Capacity Development Unit
CEE	-	Centre of Environment Education
CEO	-	Chief Executive Officer
CEP	-	Child Environment Programme
CLTS	-	Community Led Total Sanitation
CRSP	-	Central Rural Sanitation Programme
CSC	-	Community Sanitary Complex
DEO	-	District Education Officer
DFID	-	UK Department for International Development
DFT	-	Disabled Friendly Toilets
DRDA	-	District Rural Development Agency
DRP	-	District Resource Person
DWS	-	Drinking Water and Sanitation
DWSC	-	District Water and Sanitation Committee
DWSM	-	District Water and Sanitation Mission

FGD	-	Focus Group Discussion
FLHP	-	Force & Lift Hand Pumps
GOI	-	Government of India
GP	-	Gram Panchayat
GPEP	-	Gram Panchayat Environment Plan
GPU	-	Gram Panchayat Unit
HRD	-	Human Resource Development
HUDCO	-	Housing and Urban Development Corporation Limited
HWSC	-	Habitation Water & Sanitation Committee
ICDS	-	Integrated Child Development Scheme
IEC	-	Information Education and Communication
IHHL	-	Individual House Hold Latrine
ISP	-	Intensive Sanitation Project
KAP	-	Knowledge Aptitude and Practice
MDM	-	Mid Day Meal
MEO	-	Mandal Education Officer
MIS	-	Managment Information System
MRP	-	Mandal Resource Person
MS	-	Mahila Samakhya
NDDB	-	National Dairy Development Board
NFHS	-	National Family Health Survey
NGO	-	Non Governmental Organisation
NGP	-	*Nirmal Gram Puraskar* (Clean Village Award)
OA	-	Office Assistant
O & M	-	Operation and Maintenance
ODF	-	Open Defecation Free
PC	-	Production Centre
PC-SM	-	Production Coal-cum-Sanitary Mart
PHC	-	Primary Health Centre
PHE	-	Public Health Engineering
PHED	-	Public Health Engineering Department
PRA	-	Participatory Rural Apprisal
PRI	-	Panchyatai Raj Institution
PTA	-	Parent Teachers' Association
PWD	-	Public Works Department
PWDs	-	Persons With Disability
RCC	-	Reinforced Cement Concrete

RDA	-	Rural Development Assistant
RKMLP	-	Ramkrishna Mission Lokshiksha Parishad
RSM	-	Rural Sanitary Mart
RWS	-	Rural Water Supply
SAAAF Schools-Campaign		Sanitation, Awareness, Assessment and Action for Schools Campaign
SC	-	Scheduled Caste
SHG	-	Self Help Group
SIDA	-	Swedish International Development Cooperation Agency
SSHE	-	School Sanitation and Hygiene Education
ST	-	Scheduled Tribe
SUPW	-	Socially Useful Periodic Work
SWASTHH	-	School Water and Sanitation Towards Health and Hygiene
SWSM	-	State Water and Sanitation Mission
TSC	-	Total Sanitation Campaign
TV	-	Television
UNICEF	-	United Nations Children Fund
UPS	-	Upper Primary School
VDDS	-	Demand Dress Strategy
VEC	-	Village Education Committee
VHC	-	Village Health Committee
VWSC	-	Village Water and Sanitation Committee
WATSAN	-	Water and Sanitation
WB	-	World Bank
WC	-	Water Chart
WEDC	-	Water Engineering Development Centre
WES	-	Water and Environmental Sanitation
WHO	-	World Health Organisation
WQMS	-	Water Quality Monitory and Surveillance.
WQS	-	Water Quality Surveillance
WSP (SA)	-	Water and Sanitation Programme (South Asia)
ZWC	-	Zero Waste Centre
ZWM	-	Zero Waste Management

Glossary

[Above/Below] Poverty Line: The Planning Commission of the Government of India uses a food adequacy norm of 2400 to 2100 kilo calories per capita per day to define state-specific poverty lines separately for rural and urban areas. These poverty lines are then applied on India's National Sample Survey Organization's household consumer expenditure distributions to estimate the proportion and number of poor at State level.

Anganwadi: Pre-school, initiative under the Integrated Child Development Scheme of the Government of India.

ASHA: Accredited Social Health Activist appointed on honorary basis at village level under NRHM.

Block Development Officer: Key development functionary at block level serving about 100,000 population.

Central Rural Sanitation Programme: First national sanitation programme introduced by Government of India in 1986.

Chief Executive Officer: Administrative head of the District Panchayat (Zilla Panchayat).

Communication and Capacity Development Unit: Set up in each state to take up communication and capacity development activities for TSC, Swajaldhara, water quality monitoring etc. programmes supported by Government of India.

Community Led Total Sanitation: A community-wide approach based on participatory principles which seeks to achieve 100 per cent open defecation free communities.

COSTFORD: An Organisation Promoting Research in Low Cost buildings and housing.

District Water and Sanitation Mission/Committee: Separate institutional structure promoted by Government of India to implement TSC and Swajaldhara at district level.

Gram Panchayat: Local governments at the village level in India.

Information, Education, Communication: Software activities, e.g. media campaigns, capacity building activities, community hygiene promotion etc. that support and promote the programme implantation.

Integrated Child Development Scheme: A centrally sponsored Programme aimed at providing services to pre-school children in an integrated manner so as to ensure proper growth and development of children in rural, tribal and slum areas.

Intensive Sanitation Project: Community based sanitation project taken up in Midnapur district of West Bengal in early 1990s to achieve full sanitation coverage.

Mahila Samikhya: A programme for Women's Education and Empowerment.

Nirmal Gram Puraskar: Innovative Incentive Scheme launched by the Government of India for local self-governments to attain open defecation free status.

Panchayati Raj Institution: Three-tier institutions of self-governance mandated by the 73rd Constitution Amendment.

Parent Teachers' Association: Outlet for parent participation at most public and private schools.

Production Centre: Promoted under TSC to produce low cost sanitary wares.

Ram Krishna Mission Lokshiksha Parishad: Rural and social development wing of spiritual organisation Ram Krishna Mission which was set up by Swami Vivekananda.

Rural Sanitary Mart: Promoted under TSC to procure and supply sanitary wares, toilet technology and services for setting up sanitary toilets.

Scheduled Caste: Indian population groupings that are explicitly recognized by the Constitution of India, previously called the "depressed classes" by the British, and otherwise known as Harijans.

Scheduled Tribe: Indian indigenous population groupings explicitly recognized by the Constitution of India.

School Sanitation and Hygiene Education: An important component of TSC to promote sanitation and hygiene in schools and among children.

School Water and Sanitation Towards Health and Hygiene: A USAID funded project implemented by UNICEF in select districts in Jharkhand and Karnataka to promote water supply, sanitation and hygiene in schools.

Self Help Group: A group of rural poor who have volunteered to organise themselves into a group for eradication of poverty of the members.

SEVF: Socio-economic unit foundation is a voluntary organisation in the field of drinking water and sanitation.

State Water and Sanitation Mission: State level institution usually headed by the Chief Secretary to plan and monitor water supply and sanitation programmes.

Swajaldhara: A reform initiative launched by Government of India in water sector following demand driven strategy.

Total Sanitation Campaign: Revamped central rural sanitation programme launched in 1999.

Village Water and Sanitation Committee: Village level committee set up for implementation of TSC and Swajaldhara.

Zilla Panchayat: District level elected body as part of 3 tier Panchayati Raj System.

Zero Waste Management: Innovative solid waste management initiative taken up in Tamil Nadu.

List of Contributors

A.K.Singh: Deputy Director, Panchayati Raj, Govt. of Uttar Pradesh.

Amit Ghosh: IAS Officer of Uttar Pradesh Cadre.

Amit Kumar Agrawal (Dr.): IAS officer of Haryana Cadre and presently working as District Commissioner, Hisar.

Anil Mudgal: Working at Arushi, a Bhopal-based not-for-profit organization, working with and for people with disabilities and issues related to them.

C. Chandrababu: Project Director, Poverty Alleviation Unit, DRDA, Thrissur.

C.Srinivasan: President, Exnora Green Cross – Vellore, Tamil Nadu.

Chandi Charan Dey: Coordinator, Water & Sanitation, Ramakrishna Mission Lokasiksha Parishad, Narendrapur.

G. Anil : Disrict Coordinator, Total Sanitation Campaign, Thrissur.

Jai Prakash: District Coordinator, Sanitation , Medak, Andhra Pradesh.

M. Renukumar: Assitant Coordinator, Total Sanitation Campaign, Thrissur.

Md. Sadullah Jawaid: Director, PMU, Bihar State Water and Sanitation Mission, Patna.

Megha Phansalkar (Dr.): Development professional and has worked as Knowledge Management Specialist with the Water Supply and Sanitation Department, Government of Maharashtra.

Nitin Kulkarni (Dr): IAS officer of Jharkhand Cadre.

Rohit Trivedi (Dr.): Assistant Professor, Sarojini Naidu Government Girls P.G. College, Bhopal, MP.

Sanjay Dubey: Executive Engineer, Government of Bihar, Patna.

V.V.Pant: IAS officer of Uttar Pradesh Cadre.

Vishal Mukhia: Faculty, State Institute of Rural Development,Gangtok Sikkim.

Introduction

It has been 65 years since the country attained its independence; however, rural sanitation coverage still remains one of the biggest development challenges in our country. Practice of open defecation is quite rampant which is result of a combination of factors like traditional behaviour, lack of awareness of the rural masses about the health related issues, lack of priority attached to sanitation promotion etc. Successive census data related to toilet coverage and usage in rural areas have indicated very poor level of sanitation coverage resulting in large-scale unmanaged human excreta exposed in the environment leading to various water and excreta related diseases.

In this context, the first national sanitation programme in the form of Central Rural Sanitation Programme (CRSP) was launched by the Government of India in 1986 during the international decade of water supply and sanitation with the objective of improving the quality of life of the rural people and to provide privacy and dignity to women. CRSP made limited gains in accelerating sanitation coverage in rural areas. The scheme was allocation based and supply driven and did not give much emphasis on awareness creation for demand generation. Hence, it was restructured in 1999; and a demand responsive community led "Total Sanitation Campaign (TSC)" was introduced with emphasis on generating demand for sanitary facilities with extensive participation of communities. Subsequently an innovative incentive scheme "Nirmal Gram Puraskar (NGP)" was introduced in 2003 with the objective of further strengthening community participation in sanitation promotion. Nirmal Gram Puraskar is given to open defecation free Gram Panchayats, Blocks and Districts aimed at providing an impetus towards achieving full sanitation coverage in respective geographical areas. Sustained interventions from the Government and the community have showed encouraging results in several parts of our country. Sanitation coverage is estimated to have substantially increased since 2002-03. Over the years, the rural sanitation programme has witnessed a paradigm shift in the traditional approach of sanitation promotion and adopted new and innovative strategies. Gradually TSC has been able to develop various building blocks for scaling up of the programme which combined with Nirmal Gram Puraskar for the Panchayati Raj Institutions has led to a new movement sweeping across rural India.

Despite being one of the largest rural sanitation programmes in the world, the pace of implementation of TSC is not uniform across the states and districts of the country. The involvement and commitment of District and State officials also varies significantly. Even though TSC prescribes common framework for implementation throughout the country, enough flexibility has been given to the state and district functionaries and capitalizing on this many of them have adopted such approaches which deserve to be shared with other implementing agencies. This book presents thirteen case studies gathered from different states of the country covering various aspects of the Total Sanitation Campaign. These will help the district and state officials in learning from these experiences and provide them lessons to improve upon programme implementation in their respective districts/states. These case studies are written by practitioners of rural sanitation, i.e. district and state officials and NGOs directly involved in the programme implementation. They have tried to discuss the key issues, and strategies to overcome challenges citing actual case of their district or state. The book highlights key learning elements from these case studies which can be used by government officials as well as professionals working in sanitation sector and also in other social development programmes. The case studies focus on a range of issues like awareness creation and social mobilization, supply chain management, school sanitation, community participation, focus on people with special needs, monitoring and evaluation, solid and liquid waste management etc.

The first case study titled "Sanitation is a movement for Behavioural Changes: Ramakrishna Mission Lok Shiksha Parishad's Experience" written by *Shri Chandi Charan Dey* highlights the importance of Education and Awareness about sanitation amongst rural masses for internalizing the behaviour change and to adopt hygienic life style. He has drawn lessons from the experiences gained while implementing Intensive Sanitation Project and later on TSC programme in Midnapur District of West Bengal. The case study captures various processes adopted in the Midnapur sanitation movement, the institutional arrangement including synergy between NGOs and PRIs, importance of supply chain management etc. More importantly the case study clearly brings out the importance of social mobilization in sanitation promotion and establishes the fact that people are willing to construct irrespective of the quantum of subsidy given to them provided they have been made aware of the importance of sanitation for a healthy and dignified lifestyle. According to author, positive environment can be created through people's movement. He also emphasizes upon the need to inculcate the process of self-reliance and to create scope of direct participation of the people to achieve the objectives of TSC in real sense.

"Implementing CLTS in Panipat: Some Issues and Experiences" written by *A.K. Agarwal* who worked as Additional Deputy Commissioner of Panipat district and discusses the Community Led Total Sanitation (CLTS) approach in his district. Community Led Total Sanitation (CLTS) approach aims at empowering communities by making the people collectively realize that open defecation is a serious health hazard for everyone. This realization is introduced by a process called 'triggering' which initially induces behaviour change in a few people but it slowly spreads to the entire community resulting in the entire community stopping open defecation. The people build and use latrines without any external subsidy. The behaviour change so introduced, is permanent as the people have taken their own decision to stop open defecation. The author elaborates various community mobilization and social awareness generation techniques adopted while implementing TSC using CLTS approach and also analyses several issues that have emerged out of this approach which have led to creating open defecation free villages in the district.

Access is seen as a major step towards addressing the issue of marginalization of Persons with Disabilities (PWDs). The state of Madhya Pradesh alone has a total disabled population of about 1.5 million as per the census of 2001. Of these about 75 per cent reside in rural areas. Knowingly or unknowingly PWDs remain marginalized, and are often deprived of opportunities simply because schools, colleges, offices and other public places do not have accessible toilets for them. They do not move out of their houses on account of this. Particularly girls with disabilities feel embarrassed and it is a deterrent to their mainstreaming. The case study titled "Disabled Friendly Toilets in MP" written by *Shri Rohit Trivedi* and *Anil Mudgal* is based on the experiences gained by ARUSHI, a Bhopal based organization working in the field of disability. ARUSHI worked in collaboration with UNICEF on the project of *"Inclusive Models of Sanitation for Persons with Disabilities'* with the sole objective of making sanitation facilities accessible to PWDs. The project was undertaken in eight Districts of Madhya Pradesh. The purpose of this case study is to share experiential learning with TSC functionaries for inclusion of PWD in the TSC programme implementation. It highlights the special needs of the PWDs to access and use sanitation facilities.

TSC focuses on intensive social mobilization and awareness generation for creating demand for sanitation facilities. However, the demand so generated needs to be converted into construction of toilets and adoption of good hygiene behaviour. This entails that a credible delivery system in the form of rural sanitary marts or production centres remain in place in each district to meet the demand. In absence of such effective supply chain the demand generated is likely to diminish gradually. West Bengal has developed an effective supply chain in the form of Production Centres-cum-Rural Sanitary Marts in every block of the State which have established synergy among the demand generation as well as supply chain mechanism. This supply chain has been the root cause of success of the sanitation programme in West Bengal and is worth emulation by other states in the country also. The very concept of RSM in TSC has been taken from the success of Ramkrishna Mission Lokshiksha Parishad in Midnapur District which later on got scaled up in the entire West Bengal. "Production Centres-cum-Sanitary Mart: An alternate delivery mechanism for sanitation promotion in West Bengal" written by *Shri Chandi Charan Day* and

Shri Kumar Alok gives in detail the rationale and importance including various elements of an effective supply chain.

Management of solid and liquid waste is a major challenge not only in urban areas but also in the rural areas. Everyday huge volume of both organic and inorganic waste is generated in our households, shops, markets, community places etc. Unmanaged waste is on one hand a major source of diseases and on the other hand is a resource. *Mr. C. Srinivasan* has been a pioneer in developing models of solid and liquid waste management. He has successfully implemented the Zero Waste Management model in Vellore and other places in the country. He captures details of this model in the case study "Integrated and Sustainable Solid and Liquid Waste Management—Vellore Model." The author explains in detail the processes followed in Vellore model which focuses on three Rs—Reduce, Recycle and Reuse. This case study helps us understand the nature of waste, the history of waste and waste management, the different solutions already tried out and their results, and the need to turn to Zero Waste Management (ZWM). True ZWM goes beyond managing waste already generated to preventing waste generation. According to the author; Zero Waste Management project offers good opportunity for generating employment for the BPL people.

"From Sanitation to Sustainable Development: Case Study of Mahalunge village, Maharashtra" written by *Dr. Megha Phansalkar* highlights the power of community mobilization in making a village open defecation free and adopt sanitation even without any direct subsidy. The central role of community as major stakeholder in decision making and catalyst for sustainable development is fully established in this village. The village participated in the Sant Gadge Baba Abhiyan and also became a Nirmal Gram. The case study elaborates on the key aspects of Sant Gadge Baba Abhiyan launched by the Government of Maharashtra to trigger community involvement in sanitation promotion where prizes are given to Winner Panchayats. This '*abhiyan*' has been able to mobilize community action on a very large scale which is reflected in huge number of Panchayats becoming open defecation free and earning Nirmal Gram Puraskar in Maharashtra. The case study also indicates that sanitation has been a good entry point for community mobilization due to which fruits of development are reaped in other sectors also.

Women suffer the most due to absence of sanitation facilities. Mahila Samakhya (MS) in Bihar originally set up under the Bihar Education Project has played a catalytic role in mobilizing and empowering women. With a strong network and reach among women, MS has been effective in motivating women to adopt sanitation facilities. The case study written by *Mr. Jawed* highlights the key processes followed and achievements made by Mahila Samakhya in sanitation promotion in Gaya District of Bihar. The case study highlights the positive steps taken in the implementation of TSC in Gaya and the key strategies adopted by Mahila Samakhaya to earn Nirmal Gram Puraskar. It also elaborates upon the lessons learnt from various sanitation related programmes in Bihar.

The case study written by *Shri C. Chandrababu, Shri G. Anil* and *Shri M. Renukumar* titled "School Sanitation and Hygiene Education: A Case-Study of Thrissur District in Kerala" focuses on role of health clubs in schools for imparting hygiene education as well as maintaining the hardware facilities. Health Clubs in all schools were set-up which became platforms for discussions and actions on sanitation related activities. The activities of the formal Health Clubs triggered discussions and activities in informal groups of students inside as well as outside the class rooms. Training of teachers and conveners of health clubs has been a crucial element in institutionalizing the IEC activities leading to full coverage of toilets in the schools as well as their usage and maintenance. Innovative approaches for awareness creation were adopted which included sanitation ballot, quiz, cultural programme etc. According to authors, IEC in cultural mode especially street plays, skits, songs etc. attract the participation of children and facilitate learning through enjoyment. However, the campaign strategies having elements of both *mass education activities* like Kalajathas, Dramas, Paintings, Lectures, Demonstrations and *individual child centred education activities* like the monitoring card exercise, nail cutting exercise, *suchitwa* ballot are likely to be more sustainable. Authors recommend that Sanitation and Hygiene education in schools has to be a continuous education programme, otherwise the gains may not be sustainable.

Successful implementation of school sanitation and hygiene education component of TSC is possible only with the convergence of efforts of different stakeholders like community, children, teachers and panchayati raj institutions. Further water supply availability is a major pre-condition for proper upkeep of the school toilets. In order to do so dovetailing of funds under TSC and 12th Finance Commission grants have been able to bridge the resource gap. "Better School Sanitation and Hygiene Education is an effective tool to reach community" written by *Mr. V.V. Pant and Mr. A.K. Singh* highlights the initiatives taken in SSHE implementation in Varanasi district of UP focusing on various innovations in designs and convergence of resources. The case study details the story of a primary school in village Shankerpur, Block Chiraigaon in district Varanasi elaborating the processes of situational analysis, preparation of school micro plan, coordination among various officials and stakeholders and IEC activities leading to the school environment being clean and green.

Medak district in Andhra Pradesh had taken up an innovative campaign to promote school sanitation in partnership with UNICEF called 'The *SAAAF Schools Campaign*' which stands for *Sanitation, Awareness, Assessment and Action for Schools Campaign*. This campaign has brought out a new approach and new way of looking at school sanitation programme. This approach aims at assessment and action in addition to awareness only which has been a clear shift in strategy from the time when the 'soft-ware' interventions in SSHE were limited to awareness alone. The campaign has three components—(i) create awareness and to bring about attitudinal and behavioural changes among students, teachers, community and concerned line departments, (ii) Facilitate a school level assessment of the sanitation and hygiene infrastructure, use and maintenance through a participatory process involving students, teachers, head masters, community representatives and concerned line departments, and (iii) Identify and initiate action at individual, school, community and line department levels to resolve problems to ensure proper use and maintenance of WATSAN facilities. *Shri Jai Prakash* highlights the salient features of the SAAAF Schools campaign, various stakeholders and their role in the Case study on "SAAAF School Campaign" and elaborates upon the critical elements which made a difference, the challenges faced and the major outcomes of the campaign. It's clear that the schools or the concerned departments have taken school sanitation seriously. Ownership of WATSAN programme by School and community both are essential for sustainable achievement. SAAAF is a programme that has potential for replication in other districts and states as well. Mainstreaming this programme as an approach to reviving and using the existing WATSAN infrastructure in schools is necessary.

Dr. Nitin Kulkarni, the then Deputy Commissioner of East Singhbum District has captured four different types of initiatives taken in East Singhbhum District while implementing TSC in the case study "Jharkhand-Unleashing New Wave of Sanitation: A Case Study of Innovative Approaches Adopted in East Singhbhum District". The key issues discussed in this case study are: (i) Convergence of TSC with ICDS programme, (ii) Village planning for water and sanitation to influence behaviour change, (iii) Role of child cabinet in promoting school sanitation and hygiene education, and (iv) An integrated MIS to capture household level water and sanitation data for effective monitoring. According to the experience of Chakulia block in East Singhbhum, ICDS stepped in to fill the gap due to absence of NGOs and formed the backbone of the programme implementation. The case study discusses about how the success was achieved in this block and later replicated in four other blocks of the district and one of them got nominated for the NGP award during the year 2007-08. Dr. Kulkarni further highlights the importance of village planning in bringing a significant change in the quality of life through people's participation. The positive learning outcomes of this process has been that people are keen to participate but there is a need to develop strong communication with them and integrate dissemination of messages on behaviour change to help adoption. Orientation of school teachers and children on WATSAN turned into demand generation from community. The hygiene practices developed among the children under the SSHE slowly linked child to child, child to parent and parent to community. The author also highlights the important features of MIS implemented in the district to analyse key performance indicators and also to monitor the extension of water and sanitation services at household level.

Manual scavenging has been an excessively demeaning practice in Indian society which completely undermines the dignity of human beings. Despite various efforts made by the country in the form of legislation, incentive schemes for rehabilitation of scavengers etc., such practice has continued to exist for a variety of reasons.

Moradabad district in UP has been one of such districts where prevalence of dry latrines has been quite significant resulting in the existence of manual scavenging. The case study "Sanitation—A way of Life" written by *Shri Amit Kumar Ghosh* highlights the key achievements made on this front by educating people to convert their dry latrines into pour flush toilets which has automatically led to reduction in manual scavenging. Shri Ghosh presents the facts coming out of the baseline study conducted to examine and scrutinize the existing mindset and practices available. He outlines various processes followed in implementing TSC in Moradabad like planning, capacity building, role played by Information, Education and Communication (IEC) focusing on both mass media and inter-personal communication by appointing motivators, school and anganwadi sanitation etc.

Shri Vishal Mukhia's case study is based on the research study conducted to assess the impact of TSC on rural health in East and South districts of Sikkim. As per the findings of the study, TSC has been widely successful in controlling the transmission of the excreta related diseases. The sanitation technology is suggested as an additional means of combating the health problems caused by inadequate sanitation facilities. It was also found that there is significant change in the manner in which sanitation systems are chosen, designed and implemented. Also students, the next generation citizens have enough awareness about personal hygiene and use of latrines. It has also emerged from the study that the TSC has gained a lot of importance in the post-reform period. The major reason for the success of TSC is close coordination between government, community and partnership endeavours.

Compilation of these case studies has undergone a long process of selection and editing so that field functionaries implementing TSC are really benefited. All the case studies received by us were scrutinized in a workshop attended by a host of resource persons like Mr. Srikant Navrekar, Dr. S.V. Mapuskar, Mrs. Sumita Ganguly, Mr. Manu Prakash, Dr. Kamal Mazumdar, Mr. Ravi Kant Sinha and officials from LBSNAA, Mussoorie. We sincerely thank all the participants of the workshop who spared their valuable time and made their useful contributions and critical comments. This volume would never have been possibie without their valuable and active association. We deeply appreciate the efforts and support rendered by Shri Sanjeev

Sharma, Researcher, National Centre for Good Governance (*Erstwhile* National Institute of Administrative Research), Kosy Nook, Lal Bahadur Shastri National Academy of Administration, Mussoorie whose role in organizing the workshop was not only pivotal but he also provided immense assistance in preparation of the book. The shortcomings and errors in this book which remain are our alone.

Kumar Alok
A.P. Singh

1

Sanitation is a Movement for Behavioural Change

Ramakrishna Mission Lokshiksha Parishad's Experience

Chandi Charan Dey

Introduction

Safe water and sanitation are important constituents for improving the quality of life. According to the WHO, 80 per cent of diseases in our country are related to unsafe water and lack of hygiene and sanitation. About 60 per cent of the total medical expenses incurred by a family are spent for treatment of diseases arising from unsafe and poor environmental sanitation. Even after 65 years of independence, more than four lakh children (under 5 years of age) die from diseases related to contaminated water and poor sanitation.

Even as late as the 1990s, sanitation was given little importance in the development scenario of the country. Sanitation was never perceived as a priority for improving the quality of life. Although a few thousand household toilets were being constructed annually in various parts of the country but the importance of sanitation was never adequately realized in the past. Sanitation programmes in the past were conceived and implemented in the country adopting the following strategies:

- Sanitation programmes merely focused on constructing toilets rather than creating a need for the same.

- Assumed that subsidy would act as means for creating demand for household toilets.
- Allocation based programmes.
- Managed departmentally to achieve the set target.
- Highly subsidized programme for a smaller population.
- Limited community participation.
- No emphasis for awareness and capacity development of stakeholders.
- Inadequate focus on sanitation and hygiene education.

It was observed later that strategically this approach was very weak. Rather than focusing on social mobilization to create a need for toilets amongst the rural population, the earlier strategies emphasized upon target and supply driven approach which yielded nominal results. Different studies indicate that out of the total sanitary toilets constructed under various government programmes in the decade of the eighties, 50 per cent were not in use due to many reasons. Some of the important reasons for poor usage of toilets were:

- Lack of awareness on sanitation and hygiene habits,
- Poor construction standards,
- Low coverage of toilet,
- Lack of water availability for toilet use,
- Lack of scope for participation of the beneficiaries in the total process,
- Holistic view of sanitation was not taken, and
- No linkage with people and the local self-government and non-government agencies etc.

Realising the weaknesses of the ongoing sanitation initiatives in the country during the late 1980s Ramakrishna Mission Lokshiksha Parishad, Narendrapur conceived, developed and implemented a demand driven and people centred sanitation strategy for Medinipur district of West Bengal in collaboration with the Government of West Bengal, Zilla Panchayat and UNICEF. Notably, Medinipur was the most populous district of the country and its population was 8.3 million in 1991, nearly one per cent of India's population.

Demand Driven Sanitation Movement in Medinipur

Along with six other states West Bengal was selected to initiate Intensive Sanitation Programme during Water and Sanitation Decade (1981 to 1990). UNICEF being one of the partners of WATSAN Decade, requested Ramakrishna Mission Lokshiksha Parishad (RKMLP) to prepare a proposal covering a district for promotion of sanitation with innovative approaches.

First innovative sanitation promotion programme on the basis of Demand Driven Strategy (DDS) was conceived, designed and initiated in Medinipur district in the year 1990 jointly by the RKMLP and UNICEF and implemented in collaboration with the Government of West Bengal and Medinipur Zilla Parishad.

Salient Features of Medinipur Sanitation Programme

- It was a 'Demand Driven' and 'Community-Led' sanitation promotion programme. Emphasis was on intensive, area specific and time bound Information Education and Communication (IEC)/Social Mobilization activities. Specific action oriented programmes were designed and conducted for awareness generation and creation of demand for sanitation.
- Intensive Human Resource Development Programmes were designed and conducted for inculcating positive aptitude and skills for implementation of Demand Driven Sanitation (DDS) for the functionaries of Non-Government Organizations (NGOs), Community Based Organisations (CBOs), Administration and Panchayati Raj Institutions (PRIs) from district to village levels.
- Initially, it was a "No Subsidy" programme for construction of household toilets. Beneficiary families were contributing the entire cost of the toilet. In 1994, the Government of West Bengal introduced a backend incentive of Rs. 200 for each BPL family for construction of household toilets.
- As there was no provision of subsidy and people were neither much willing nor had means to invest for toilet construction, RKMLP developed different affordable technological options

for household toilets with upgradation facilities. Six different cost effective household toilet models with cost ranging from Rs. 230 to Rs. 3,000[1] (in 1990) were offered to the families to choose as per their economic affordability.

- An alternative delivery network was developed by establishing Production Centre-cum-Sanitary Marts in each block involving Cluster Organizations of RKMLP. 25 Sanitary Mart-cum-Production Centres in *Purab Medinipur* and 29 such centres in *Paschim Medinipur* district were established.
- A network of voluntary workers (sanitation motivators) was developed involving associated village youth clubs and Gram Panchayats. Incentive of motivators was linked with the physical achievement.
- For the first time in the country a Voluntary Organization was made a Nodal Agency for implementing Sanitation project in a district while the District Administration and Panchayati Raj Institutions (PRIs) extended necessary support in implementation of Sanitation Programme.
- A systematic weekly monitoring mechanism involving all sectors was developed to monitor the progress and to overcome the shortcomings.
- This was the first sanitation project in the country, which had been initiated in a movement-mode for promotion of sanitation.

Programme Implementation Mechanism

All development programmes of RKMLP are implemented through its associated village youth clubs and cluster organizations (Federation of associated village youth clubs of RKMLP) under the guidance and technical support of the Parishad. RKMLP has developed a strong network involving more than 1100 village youth clubs and 21 cluster organizations for decentralized programme planning, implementation and monitoring of all its development activities.

Implementation Infrastructure

A three-tier implementation infrastructure was created in Medinipur for effective implementation of Sanitation promotion activities. A schematic diagram of the institutional structure is shown in Figure 1.1.

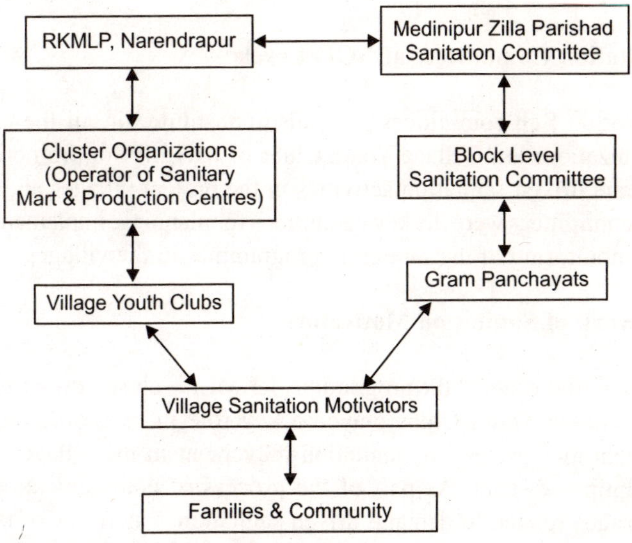

Fig. 1.1: Institutional Structure of Medinipur Sanitation Project

District Sanitation Committee

A District level Sanitation Committee was constituted under the Chairmanship of Zilla Parishad *Sabhadhipati* (Chairperson). Other members of the committee were District Magistrate, Representative of RKMLP, Representative of UNICEF, Karmadhyaksha, *Janaswasthya Paribesh* Sthayee Samiti of Zilla Parishad, District Panchayat Officer, District Chief Medical Officer of Health and Additional Executive Officer of Zilla Parishad. The role of this committee was to provide guidance and policy support for smooth implementation of "Community Led and Demand Driven" sanitation promotion strategy, that had been conceived and designed by RKMLP.

Block and Gram Panchayat Sanitation Committee

Similarly, Sanitation Committees were constituted involving the Block level Development Officials and Panchayat functionaries, Pradhans of Gram Panchayats, cluster organizations and Village Youth Clubs of RKMLP in all the project blocks and Gram Panchayats in the district.

Sanitation Committees at NGO Levels

Sanitation Sub-committees were also constituted in all the cluster organizations and Village Youth Clubs of RKLMP for promotion of demand driven sanitation activities in the project villages and these sub-committees were the key institutions for planning, implementation and monitoring of the sanitation programmes in the villages.

Network of Sanitation Motivators

In the initial years of the programme, RKMLP's cluster organizations and Village Youth Clubs played a key role in spreading the new concept and strategy of sanitation movement in the villages under Medinipur district. As part of the process of communication, the messages related to demand driven sanitation, a network of trained sanitation motivators was created. For every 200-250 families, one village youth (male or female) was selected by the Village Youth Clubs and trained by the RKMLP to promote sanitation and hygiene education in all the villages. These trained sanitation motivators were attached with the village youth clubs to regularly interact with the families at household level. Door to door visits comprised the main strategy for communicating sanitation education and creating demand for toilet and other sanitary facilities. RKMLP's associated cluster organizations and Village Youth Clubs along with their trained sanitation motivators were the key factors for successful grounding of "Demand Driven and Self-Financed" sanitation concept in the remote rural areas and establishing this as movement for change.

Youths and Women are the Key Force

Youth has always played the role of Key Change Agent. This has once again been proved in Medinipur Sanitation Movement where the young men and women of various villages were successful in stopping the age-old habits of open defecation through this sanitation movement. To make the youth and youth organizations aware about the needs of demand driven and self-financed sanitation concept and its impact on human health and society, a series of orientation programmes were organized by the RKMLP in the beginning of the programme. As a result of this endeavour, a large number of village youth clubs participated spontaneously in the movement. In the beginning (during 1990) only 125 village youth clubs were involved in the programme, but within two years about 1100 more village youth clubs joined the movement along with about 40,000 volunteers.

Technology Options for Toilet Models

The major objective of Medinipur Sanitation Programme was to change the mindset and the attitude of the people in order to motivate them to use toilets and to stop the practice of open defecation. RKMLP conducted a study to assess the Knowledge, Attitude and Practice (KAP) towards sanitation and hygiene practices of the people of Medinipur district in the initial stage of the programme for developing the implementation strategies, IEC activities and IEC materials for awareness generation. The study revealed that almost all the families had a positive attitude towards cash investment between Rs. 200-600 for construction of a household toilet. Considering this attitude RKMLP designed, developed and demonstrated six different toilet models and offered to the people. RKMLP developed the toilet models keeping in view the following aspects:

- Habits and cultural practices of the people
- Cash investment attitude of the families
- Comfort of the people.

Before Medinipur Sanitation Programme, such options were not offered in any sanitation promotion initiatives in the country. It was observed in Medinipur's demand driven sanitation programme that even high income group families were also opting for the lowest cost toilet model in the beginning. After using the toilets for few years and developing a habit of toilet use they upgraded their toilet units through the services of a network of trained masons of Sanitary Marts operated by the RKMLP's cluster organisations.

Institutionalization of Supply System

One of the basic objectives of Medinipur sanitation movement was demand generation for sanitation facilities through intensive awareness generation and social mobilization programmes. Along with demand generation for sanitation facilities it is very much important to develop a regular supply chain mechanism to cater to the demand by providing the necessary hardware and ancillary services. RKMLP thus developed a supply chain network establishing Production Centre-cum-Rural Sanitary Marts (PC-RSM) in each block involving Cluster Organizations of RKMLP. The PC-RSM is an institutional network from where the motivated families can procure all the materials required for installation of toilet, improved smokeless *chullahs*, bathing platform etc. and also get skilled manpower. PC-RSMs produce mosaic pans and traps, concrete platforms, doors and pit-covers etc. which are provided to the families on payment. 25 such Production Centre-cum-Sanitary Marts in Purab Medinipur and 29 in Paschim Medinipur district were established to cater to the demand for construction of sanitation facilities. Village Sanitation Motivators act as local contact persons for Sanitary Marts.

Presently the network of sanitary mart is being used for promotion of National Water Quality Monitoring and Surveillance system. Water Testing Laboratories are established in the sanitary marts. Motivators attached with the sanitary marts are facilitating the collection of water samples from the villages and generating awareness on safe water. An innovative community based water quality monitoring and surveillance system has been demonstrated by the sanitary marts in the selected Gram Panchayats.

Demand Generation Process

Demand generation for sanitation facilities was the basic goal of the sanitation programme in Medinipur. Due to a very high subsidy regime prevailing during 1990s demand generation for self-financed household toilet construction and for other sanitation facilities was a very difficult task. At that time almost all the development programmes implemented by the Government Departments or by the NGOs were highly subsidized. Under the Central Rural Sanitation Programme (CRSP) there was even a provision of a subsidy of Rs. 2000 for the construction of household toilets for BPL and SC/ST families. In that situation RKMLP's initiative of self-financed sanitation programme posed a real challenge. RKMLP was very much aware about the ground situations and accordingly developed few innovative strategies to operationalise the idea of demand creation for self-financed household sanitation facilities. The basic strategies were—

- *Area concentrated approach:* Initially only few villages were identified to demonstrate the result. As a result of this approach, 4 villages were able to achieve 100 per cent toilet coverage in all households within 9 months and inspired by this experience, 24 more villages achieved 100 per cent toilet access status in the second year. Area concentrated approach continued and by the end of fourth year of the movement 3 Gram Panchayats and 87 villages could achieve the status of 'open defecation free villages' without any subsidy incentive. 1,23,000 families installed household toilets sharing the total cost in first 4 years.
- *Time bound programme:* An intensive awareness drive was conducted for nearly 6 months to get the positive result.
- *Involving youth and youth organizations:* Village Youth Clubs and the youth were involved in this programme as sanitation motivators, playing the role of change agents. Youth clubs played a major role in motivating the families and initiated the campaign for promoting access to toilets for all village households.
- *Intensive awareness generation activities:* The aim of awareness generation activities was to change the mindset of people and to discourage open defecation practices while motivating the people to adopt the use of toilets. So intensive awareness generation activities were designed and implemented in the target villages. Major emphasis was on door to door campaign which was carried by trained

sanitation motivators and a group of youth club functionaries. Apart from this, Focused Group Discussions were also a major component of awareness generation campaign. In addition, a large number of mass communication programmes for awareness generation including songs, videos and slide shows, drama, exhibitions, rally, wall writings, hoardings etc. were organized to create a positive atmosphere towards safe sanitation movement.

- *Empowering women:* Defecating in open is a major problem faced by women in the thickly populated areas. Considering the concerns of women their direct involvement was ensured through their empowerment. 30 per cent of sanitation motivators were women. Women were visiting families to motivate them to install and use toilets. About 140 Women were trained as Masons and were engaged in production of sanitary wares.
- *Involvement of Panchayats:* Promotion of sanitation is one of the basic responsibilities of the Panchayati Raj Institutions. Proper emphasis was given on orientation and involvement of the PRI members for promotion of demand driven sanitation from the initiation of the programme. Panchayat members were also visiting the families to motivate them to install and use the toilets.

IEC Materials Developed by RKMLP for Promotion of Sanitation

RKMLP developed different types of Information Education and Communication (IEC) materials to cater to the needs of the programme. The field functionaries of the programme contributed a lot in developing content of the IEC materials. The following IEC materials were developed:

1. Hand Book on Sanitation for field functionaries (in Bengali and in English).
2. Question Answer Book on Sanitation for field functionaries.
3. Flash Cards on Sanitation and Hygiene.
4. Technical Drawing, Design Book on production and Construction of Sanitation facilities.

5. Two Posters on two different themes.
6. Folder on Sanitation promotion.
7. Leaflets on (a) Control of Diarrhoeal Diseases and (b) Need for a Toilet in Home.
8. Audio Cassette with 10 Songs on Sanitation and Water.
9. Three features based on motivational Video Films on Sanitation:
   - *Jeevan Patua*
   - *Aar Deri Noy*
   - *Mukti.*
10. Pictorial Calendar on Sanitation and Hygiene practice.
11. Banner on different toilet designs and scope of upgradation, hygiene message.

Key Achievements

Medinipur Sets a New Path

Medinipur Demand Driven Sanitation Strategy (DDSS) has been able to set a new path for promotion of Rural Sanitation activities in West Bengal. Medinipur Sanitation strategy has been recognized as a 'Role Model' for promotion of Central Rural Sanitation Programme (CRSP) in India. Government of India accepted almost all the principles, strategies and methodologies developed and practiced in Medinipur Sanitation Programme in order to implement the countrywide Total Sanitation Campaign (TSC) programme under CRSP.

Salient Physical Achievements in Medinipur

- As a result of this intensive endeavour, household toilet coverage increased to 100 per cent in Purab Medinipur (total households 7,83,623) and 98 per cent in Paschim Medinipur (total households: 9,14,042) district in December 2008, against 4.74 per cent in 1991.
- It was noticed that the incidence of diarrhoeal diseases has tremendously reduced in the 100 per cent toilet access blocks and Gram Panchayats.
- Out of a total 7376 Rural Primary Schools of Purab and

Paschim Medinipur districts, school toilet blocks installed in all 7376 Primary Schools till December 2006.

- Nandigram-II Block of Purab Medinipur district is the first block in the country which has achieved 100 per cent household toilet coverage in December 2001.
- Presently all 25 blocks of Purab Medinipur district have achieved 100 per cent household toilet coverage and the district has applied for "Nirmal Zilla Puraskar".
- More than 30 International delegations from China, Vietnam, Bangladesh, Pakistan, Sri Lanka, Indonesia, Burma, Nepal, Nigeria, Tanzania, South Africa, Zimbabwe and International Aid Agencies (UNICEF, WHO, DFID, SIDA, AUS-Aid, Water Aid, World Bank-WSP etc.) made study tours to understand the innovative approach and strategies developed and practised in Medinipur Demand Driven Sanitation Programme.
- High-level delegations consisting of Ministers, Principal Secretaries, Engineering Heads of PHED/Water Boards, State Nodal Officers of Sanitation etc. from almost all the States of India have visited Medinipur Sanitation Programme.
- Government of West Bengal is regularly using the expertise and infrastructure of RKMLP for imparting various training and orientation programmes for the TSC functionaries in West Bengal.

Medinipur Sanitation created Scope of Income Generation too

16,56,637 cost effective household toilets were installed in Purab and Paschim Medinipur districts through Production Centre-cum-Sanitary Marts run by the Cluster Organisations of RKMLP. 648 Masons (296 Men and 352 Women) were engaged for production of RCC Plate and Mosaic Pan and Traps in 54 production centres. One of the most encouraging facts is that gradually local employment, manufacturing and marketing sector has been developed around home toilet items, virtually an unwanted commodity previously.

It is observed that all the masons engaged in production activities have put their children in the school. Almost all the women masons have opened recurring deposit accounts in the nearby Banks/Post

Offices. They are utilizing their earnings for education and nutritional supplement of the children, construction of houses and towards starting small business for economic rehabilitation of their grown up sons and daughters.

A sum of Rs. 11,31,09,278 has been paid to the masons and Motivators as wages and incentives directly from the production process of sanitary wares produced at local level.

Community based Maintenance System in Drinking Water Sources

RKMLP is also directly involved in drinking water supply programme for more than two decades. Community based Maintenance System in drinking water sources—conceived and practiced by the Parishad—has been appreciated by different agencies. Parishad installed 800 Hand Pumps in Medinipur and 120 Hand Pumps in Bankura, South 24 Parganas and North 24 Parganas districts. The community maintains all these Hand Pumps. A Water Users' Committee with 7 members has been formed for each hand pump, and water users' families are contributing 10-12 rupees annually towards the operation and maintenance of the hand pumps. Two trained village women are voluntarily doing the maintenance job. This strategy influenced Medinipur Zilla Parishad to introduce Community based Maintenance System for the Hand Pumps installed by the Panchayats.

Water Quality Surveillance Programme

In recent years water quality has got the priority in the development sector. RKMLP has taken up Water Quality Surveillance (WQS) activities as one of its integrated development initiatives. As a part of WQS programme, the Parishad has established 17 Water Quality Testing Laboratories including one Laboratory in the premises of RKMLP at Narendrapur with the support of Government of West Bengal and UNICEF for testing of Arsenic, Fluoride and other parameters of drinking water. 14 Labs are working in Purab and Paschim Medinipur districts and 3 are in South 24 Parganas. Awareness generation towards safe water and its management and water sample collection was carried out with the help of the sanitation network developed in these districts. PRI bodies are using the facilities of these Labs for testing of public drinking water sources. Even private tube well owners are also availing these facilities.

Demonstration of Community Managed Water Quality Monitoring and Surveillance (WQMS)

RMKLP has demonstrated community managed WQMS systems in 14 Gram Panchayats of Purab and Paschim Medinipur districts. 950 Water Ussers' groups and 14 Gram Panchayat level Water Users' Federation have been developed and empowered. All the member families of water users' committees are contributing a sum of Rs. 12 annually towards the WQMS programme. From this contribution water is tested from the Labs and minor repairing of water sources is undertaken. So far Rs. 36,000 have been deposited in the chest fund in 8 months period.

Linking Sanitation with Carbon Credit

RKMLP has facilitated 4000 families to install and regularly use toilet link biogas plants in Medinipur and Nadia districts of West Bengal. RKMLP has initiated a project to claim carbon credits for these 4000 toilet link Biogas plants with an objective for encouraging the villagers to adopt the Biogas plant to manage all the households generated bio-degradable waste at site. For this purpose, RKMLP has registered itself as 'Aggregator' with Chicago Climate Exchange to facilitate these households to claim carbon credits.

Development of Iron and Arsenic Removal Filter

In collaboration with UNICEF, a cost effective Iron and Arsenic Removal Filter has been developed and social marketing is being done through the Sanitary Mart network in West Bengal. These filters are very efficient for removing Arsenic and Iron from the drinking water. Cost of Arsenic removal filter and Iron removal filter comes to Rs. 450 and Rs. 250 respectively. The Government of West Bengal and UNICEF have entrusted the Parishad for providing technical training for production of filters and social marketing support for promotion of the filters to the Sanitary Marts of West Bengal for promotion of Iron and Arsenic removal filters in the State. RKMLP is regularly holding seminars, group meetings, inter-personal contact drives on water quality and surveillance in the villages.

Recognition by the Government of India

- Medinipur Demand Driven Sanitation Strategy has been recognized as 'Role Model' for promotion of CRSP (Central Rural Sanitation Programme) in India.
- On recognition of pivotal contribution to Sanitation Movement the Department of Drinking Water Supply, Government of India had included Ramakrishna Mission Lokasiksha Parishad, Narendrapur in the following committees of Central Rural Sanitation Programme—
  - National Scheme Sanctioning Committee for Total Sanitation Campaign (TSC) Programme,
  - National Review Mission for TSC and Swajaldhara Programmes, and
  - National Screening Committee for Nirmal Gram Puraskar
- Department of Drinking Water Supply, Ministry of Rural Development, Government of India recognized Ramakrishna Mission Lokshiksha Parishad, Narendrapur as one of four key resource Institutes in the year 2004-05 for Capacity Development of key functionaries of Total Sanitation Campaign (TSC) programme.
- RKMLP's Sanitation experiments have been documented by different National and International Agencies for the benefit of others. One such documentation has been done by eminent writer Maggie Black with Rupert Talbot and published from OXFORD University Press in 2005.

National Award

Department of Drinking Water Supply, Ministry of Rural Development of Government of India awarded prestigious "Nirmal Gram Puraskar" to Ramakrishna Mission Lokshiksha Parishad of Ramakrishna Mission Ashrama, Narendrapur in recognition of its commendable contribution to promotion of rural sanitation programmes in the country. In a function, organised by the Department of Drinking Water Supply in the Vigyan Bhavan, New Delhi, Hon'ble Dr. A.P.J. Abdul Kalam, President of India handed over the award to Swami Asaktananda, Secretary of the Ashrama on 23rd March, 2006.

It's a Humble Beginning

Sanitation is not a programme, it is a process for internalizing and practicing the new life style. Education and awareness generation are the basic tools to help people internalize the process and adopt the new hygienic life style. RKMLP has initiated the process of inculcating the concept of self-reliance amongst the rural masses by involving them in the total process. This process is a time taking one. We have been able to develop a positive environment through people's movement. We need to nurture the environment. It has started giving some results. In an informal study it has been revealed that 76 per cent households of Medinipur want to upgrade their cost effective toilet and 38 per cent households want to upgrade the toilet with ceramic tiles floor. It is obviously an indicator that people of Medinipur have accepted the practice of using the toilet and want to sustain this habit. But we have to initiate these programmes for sustainable management of solid and liquid waste by increasing community participation. Trusting upon the strength of the people and community, sustainability of the movement can be ensured.

Swami Vivekananda had advised to educate the people on various aspects at their door step and to provide them opportunities to take the decisions for their own developmental aspects. He has emphasised in his writings that even if the entire wealth of the world is poured in a village but if the people of the village do not want to change themselves, no development can take place. Sanitation initiatives of the RKMLP have attempted to inculcate the process of self-reliance and to create scope of direct participation for the people to put in practice the teachings of Swamiji and also achieved success to a large extent. We are to go a long way to make it sustainable and to practice this process in other spheres of development initiatives.

NOTE

1. Cost based on 1990 prices.

2

Implementing Community Led Total Sanitation in Panipat

Some Issues and Experiences

Amit K. Agrawal

Panipat district situated in the state of Haryana is well known as the venue for three famous historical battles which had a major influence on the course of Medieval Indian history. In modern times, Panipat is well known internationally for handloom textiles, draperies, upholsteries and other furnishing materials. Although Panipat is a small district in terms of geographical area, it has a sizeable population of over one million.

Although Haryana[1] is one of the most prosperous and economically sound states of the country, sanitation has usually been a neglected area over the years. This can largely be attributed to lack of consciousness regarding sanitation among the people at large and also due to lack of political will over the issue. Widespread practice of open defecation in rural areas due to poor access to toilets has had a very adverse impact on health of communities in terms of diseases like diarrhoea, jaundice, worm infestation, cholera etc. A programme sponsored by Government of India called "Total Sanitation Campaign (TSC)", which aims at improving sanitation in rural areas by focusing on construction of individual and community toilets, solid and liquid waste management etc. was being implemented since 2005. However, the focus was on providing subsidies to the people Below Poverty Line (BPL) to construct individual and community toilets. There was not much effort on IEC (Information, Education and Communication) up to collect baseline data regarding availability and use of toilets and other practices related to sanitation. The aim of this survey was to collect authentic baseline data to monitor progress and to establish a rapport between the community and the CLTS team. Every single household was visited, and after filling the questionnaire a small gift of ladel[3] was given and the household was requested to come to a central place in the village at an appointed hour. No advice regarding open defecation or any other sanitary habit was given at this stage. This small gift created a rapport between the team and the community and this way we ensured good participation of the community during 'triggering' process and also people were more receptive to the team's ideas. Another benefit of use of ladel was prevention of contamination of drinking water by dipping of fingers.

After the villagers collected at some central place at the appointed hour, the process of triggering was carried out using various tools and techniques like transect walk, faecal mapping, assessment of quantity of shit produced by the village etc. The team of volunteers would take the villagers through a transect walk of the village and they would stop in places where people defecate openly and talk about issues related to health and sanitation. Most of the times the villagers were very embarrassed to stay at these dirty and smelly spots in front of outsiders, and they attempted to move the volunteers from these areas. However, the more the community tried to move away from such spots, the more the volunteers stopped at such places and asked discomforting questions about open defecation and diseases prevalent in the community. This embarrassment experienced by the community during this walk led to strong feeling of stopping open defecation to clean up such dirty spots, so as to avoid future embarrassment on subsequent visit of the outsiders. A mapping exercise with the villagers was also done where all the households were marked and people practicing open defecation were asked to mark common places of open defecation. The villagers then also calculated the amount of faeces being contributed by them per day, per week, per month and then per year which came to more than 200 tonnes for a village where 1200 people go out for defecation. Defecation maps were prepared which show how this huge quantity of faeces ultimately finds its way to their food and water.

This instilled in the villagers a sense of shock and disgust and three-fourth of the time, the village collectively decided to come out of this sorry situation by taking collective action within a short and specified period of time (this timeline was decided by the villagers themselves). During this process many community leaders also emerged who took the onus of working for the community and to motivate the entire community to get rid of this bad habit. After this a committee of villagers was formed which consisted of community leaders, Sarpanch[4], ex-sarpanch, other opinion makers of the community and some other village level government functionaries which included teacher of the local school and village level health functionary. This committee has been called the *Village Water and Sanitation Committee*. Here it is pertinent to mention that the process of formation of committee takes place before the entire community and then they are asked to formulate a rough plan for taking the village to ODF status before the community itself. The idea of formation of committee was to systematize the process of taking the community to ODF status and at the same time involving the community by having a core team from the community itself which takes the responsibility, chalks out a plan, and helps in creating community pressure on people who still refuse to stop open defecation. To further strengthen the committee, a bank account was opened for every committee and some funds (Rs. 5,000 initially) were transferred to this account from "Total Sanitation Campaign" programme. The committee could use these funds for carrying out IEC activities in the village, to appoint village level motivators on a nominal honorarium who would go from house to house to motivate people to stop going in the open to defecate. These committees were also encouraged to carry out activities like mass plantation drives, painting competition, debates etc. among school children to send a message to the community and to bind the community together. IEC activities like street plays on themes of sanitation, inspirational movies of success stories of other villages have been developed which is provided to the committees as per their demand.

Once the triggering is accomplished and committee is constituted, the team of coordinators moves to another village. On an average, it takes around 5-7 days to accomplish this task for a single village. However, the role of coordinators does not end here. Each cluster coordinator (for 5-6 villages) also acts as the Member Secretary and fact this was the biggest challenge that we faced. Rural population in Haryana is used to receive big subsidies from Central as well as the State Governments for various purposes from individual houses to water supply, electricity and all developmental works in the villages. Water and electricity are practically free for the farmers, and they do not have to pay any tax including income tax. Such an environment over the years has created a psyche of complete dependence on the government for everything. It has also undermined the community feeling as there are few issues on which people have to come together or work together. We had to declare that all subsidies for toilets have been withdrawn before we could even introduce CLTS. We are practically working in contravention of government guidelines and not providing subsidies even after they have constructed toilets.

5. *Isolated and small communities* are more amenable to CLTS than larger ones and the communities which are closer to towns. Similarly, communities which have poor socio-economic status have better rate of success in CLTS than their more forward counterparts.
6. *Role of community leaders and natural leaders* has been quite important. In communities where leaders were highly motivated, they acted as catalysts for the entire process. In many instances some of them were so enthusiastic that they even helped the community in procuring toilet construction materials in bulk on their own.
7. This approach heavily depends on *quality as well as motivation of facilitators* and volunteers and their capacity to influence the society.
8. Some kind of *institutional structure* like formation of village water and sanitation committee, coordinators at various levels has helped in giving CLTS a direction and we can proceed in a planned way and also set quantifiable targets like number of ODF communities added. An institutional mechanism might also help in maintaining the ODF status and it also helps administrators in monitoring progress.
9. CLTS has a huge potential for *self-spreading*. In Panipat, most of the coordinators are people who have played an

environment. In Indian context, the *Persons with Disabilities (Equal Opportunities, Protection of Rights and Full Participation) Act, 1995*, (*PWD Act)*, also calls for creation of barrier free environment. However, at the implementation level, not much has been achieved. Barrier-free environment, when present in buildings, is limited to ramps that too without actually meeting the needs of the PWDs. The drawback that comes in the way of creating a barrier free environment is lack of awareness, sensitivity and lack of positive attitudes on the part of the community in general and policy makers and implementing agencies in particular. Further, people with disabilities are low on the priority list when any development activity is being planned. The same has been the fate of the Total Sanitation Campaign (TSC) in its implementation so far.

Madhya Pradesh is witnessing a transformation in terms of sanitation by vigorously implementing the campaign for total sanitation. But, can the so called TSC be called *TOTAL* without taking into account PWDs, who constitute a sizeable population? Therefore, *Arushi* in collaboration with *UNICEF* implemented a project titled *"Inclusive models of sanitation for persons with disabilities"*.

The Project

The objective of the project was to create socially inclusive models of sanitation for Persons with Disabilities. The project was designed to achieve the following :

- Create awareness about the needs of "Persons with Disabilities" to access basic services.
- Develop engineering designs for wider use.
- Create access to "Disable Friendly Toilets (DFT)" at major public locations as models.

Approach and Methodology

In the first phase, the plan was to develop DFTs catering to individual households and schools both in rural and urban areas in eight districts, i.e. Guna, Shivpuri, Dhar, Jhabua, Mandsore, Sehore, Dewas and Bhopal. The second phase involved child friendly toilets and toilet complexes in Anganwadi Centres of Guna and Shivpuri districts with special emphasis on the needs of disabled children. These districts are marked out in the map of M.P. given in Figure 3.1.

As a first step, a study was undertaken to define the special needs of PWDs with respect to sanitation facilities. This was felt essential that given the diverse needs of each type of impairment, which can be broadly classified into four categories, viz. locomotor, visual, mental, speech and hearing impairment. Keeping the diverse needs in mind, the objective of the study was two fold:

(a) To understand the various problems faced by PWDs in accessing sanitation facilities in home and at public places,
(b) To develop designs and features that can make toilets disabled friendly.

Strategy and Activities

A multi-pronged strategy was adopted focusing on all stakeholders, viz. PWDs, community, the government machinery, planners, engineers, architects and masons who were to construct the DFTs. It envisaged the following:

(a) Need assessment.
(b) Organize awareness and sensitization programmes on socially inclusive models of sanitation involving all those responsible for planning and implementation of TSC in the Government machinery.
(c) Link with relevant agencies to develop designs for DFTs and simultaneously developing need based designs of accessible toilets by involving the experts.
(d) Develop and compile designs into a manual.
(e) Orientation and training of Masons.
(f) Identification of locations for DFTs.
(g) Construction of DFTs at major public locations. It was decided to select twenty prominent locations that would serve as models.
(h) Low cost technology alternatives.

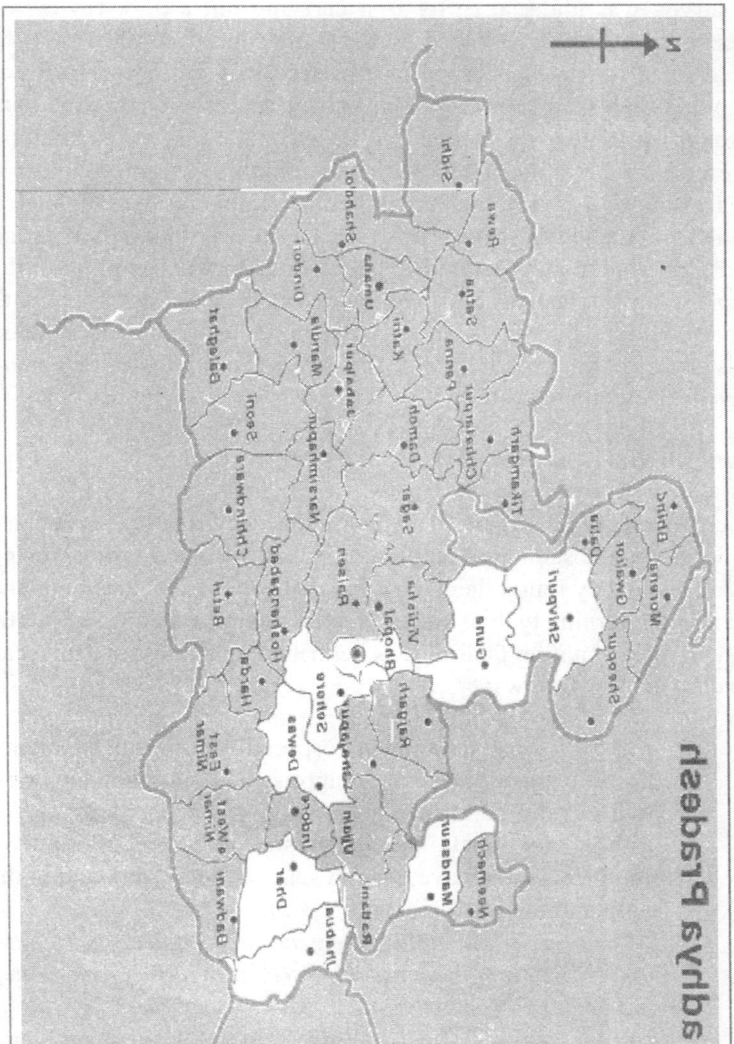

Fig. 3.1: Project Intervention Districts in M.P.

Survey

A survey was undertaken by first carrying out a desk review of secondary literature followed by a sample survey of 100 PWDs to understand the problems they face in accessing sanitation facilities in public and private places. The survey captured qualitative data through open ended questionnaires. Based on the answers, simulation exercises were undertaken with participants, to gain a clearer understanding of the problems. The participants also suggested remedies to tackle these problems. The survey was done in both urban and rural area in and around Bhopal city. A random sampling of the target group was carried out covering all categories of disability, with representatives from both urban and rural areas. Due consideration was given to women participants. The survey also attempted to broadly cover different age groups.

Data Analysis and Findings

The general response from PWDs was that they required assistance to access public sanitation facilities. Girls and women avoided using them, since they found them too cumbersome and embarrassing and preferred returning to their homes. The challenging features of public and private sanitation facilities, as described by the respondents, can be classified as follows:

(a) *Approach*: Most respondents, especially those with locomotor disability mentioned that the approach to sanitation facilities, both in rural and urban areas was very poor. Steps were a problem for most. They suggested ramps as alternative. Entrance should have enough space for accommodating the ramp and the handrail (Figure 3.2).
In rural areas the Toilets are generally located out side the house. The example shows the entrance modified with a ramp and grab rail to be used by a disabled person.

(b) *Entrance/Door:* Wheelchair users, at times, faced problems in accessing the facility due to narrow toilet doors, preventing entry on wheelchair. If the door opened inwards, it was difficult to close the door with wheelchair inside. In absence

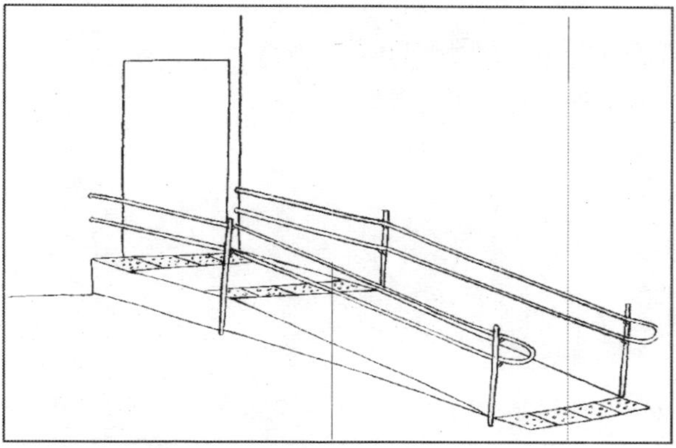

Fig. 3.2: Entrance with a Ramp

of support, they found it cumbersome to open and shut the door from a wheelchair.

Opening of door from either side could be facilitated by attaching a rope/string from the door to the grab rail (Figure 3.3).

(c) *Direction:* The visually impaired often faced problems in finding directions to and inside the sanitation facility. Tactile ground surface indicators for the blind help orientate them to the location of toilets. These must be properly placed and maintained as warning tiles (Figure 3.4).

Warning tiles are difficult to get in rural areas. Glass marble (kanchi) and river pebbles of suitable sizes are good alternatives.

(d) *Alarm system:* The disabled felt the need for a bell to attract attention in emergency. (Figure 3.5).

(e) *Signage:* The signage displaying availability and accessibility need to be displayed for PWDs (Figures 3.6 and 3.7).

(f) *Water Closet (WC) Cubicle:* Wheelchair users cited examples where the wheelchair would not fit into a WC cubicle nor was there enough space for wheelchair movement. Indian style (squat) toilets were totally inaccessible (Figure 3.8).

(g) *Support features:* A general need was felt for handrail support inside the toilet, near the WC and wash-basin (Figure 3.9).

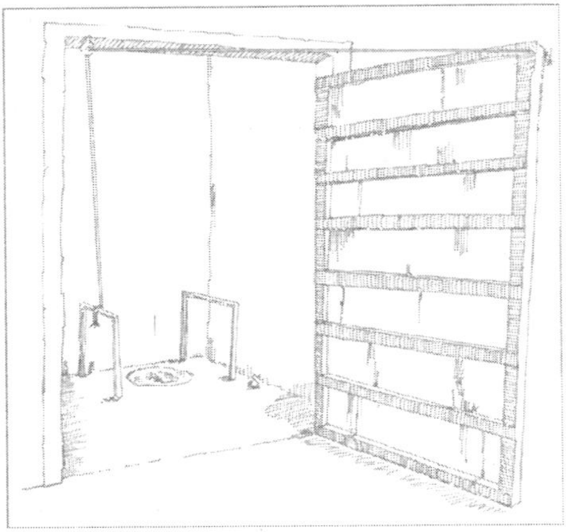

Fig. 3.3: Use of Rope for Opening/Closing the Door

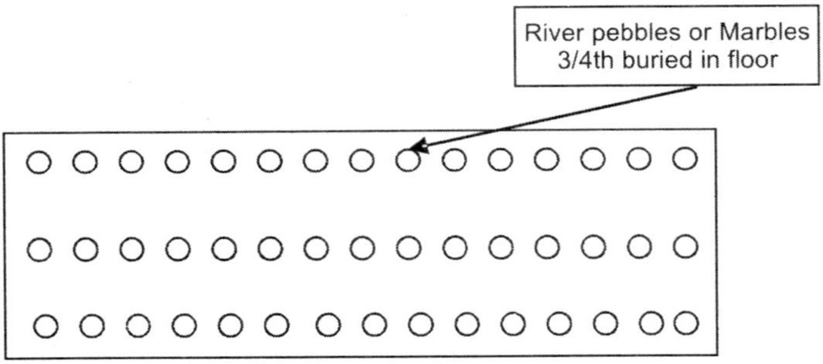

Fig. 3.4: Warning Tiles

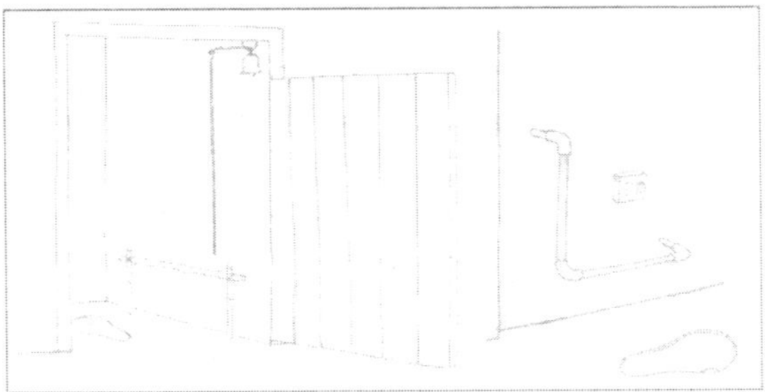

Fig. 3.5: Alarm Systems

Fig. 3.6: Toilets are Available that have been Adapted for People with Mobility Impairments

Fig. 3.7: The Premises are Fully Accessible for Wheelchair Users

(h) *Miscellaneous:*

- Wheelchair users found wash-basins too high.
- In some cases there was no clear floor space in front of the basin for wheelchair user.
- Some parents felt the need for an alarm bell inside the toilet in emergency.
- Slippery floors were a problem in most public toilets.
- Inaccessibility of mirrors for wheelchair users.
- In a couple of cases, the persons showed inability to open regular taps.

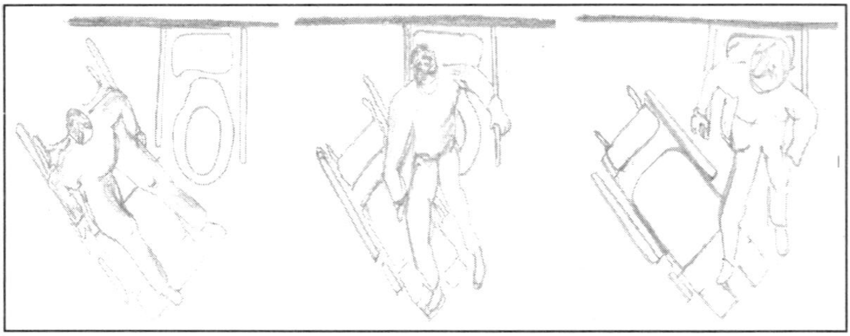

Steps for Side transfer from Wheel chair to the WC

Step 1 Step 2 Step 3

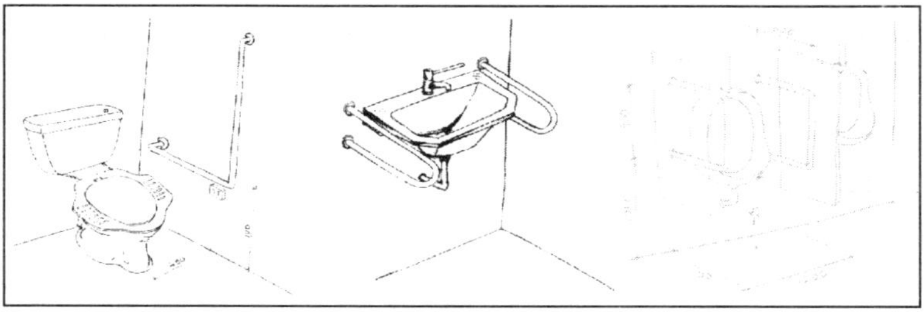

Fig. 3.8: Toilets are Available that have been Adapted for People with Mobility Impairments

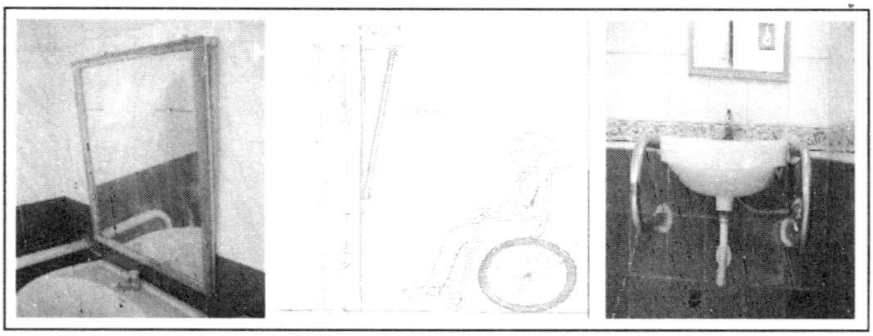

Fig. 3.9

Workshops and Programmes: Awareness and sensitization programmes on inclusive models of sanitation were organized with different stakeholders like officials and agencies involved in the implementation of TSC or engaged in infrastructure development at the District, State, National and International level. The aim of these programmes was to sensitize them towards the need for accessibility features in buildings, with special focus on disabled friendly toilets. These programmes were designed to make participants experience the problems faced by PWDs. For this, simulation exercises were undertaken with the participants with activities like making them move blindfolded or on a wheelchair. During these programmes, all aspects of disabled friendly toilets were discussed. The senior officials of different engineering departments realized that such designs should be developed and be made available easily, so that accessibility issues could be addressed and government departments could adopt these models. It was also suggested that these designs should be developed for both urban and rural areas and should cater for households and public places. Low cost technology options for rural toilets were also offered (Fig. 3.10).

Manual development: Arushi, with the help of specialists including architects, experts on disability, water and sanitation experts, developed designs of disabled friendly toilets and brought out a manual. This manual covers designs of DFTs for public places, schools, and households in rural and urban setting. Low cost alternatives are also covered. Locally available inexpensive construction material (e.g. bamboo) in place of standard material can reduce the cost of construction by more than 40 per cent (Fig. 3.11).

The manual covers the following aspects: DFT:

(a) General principles of accessibility.

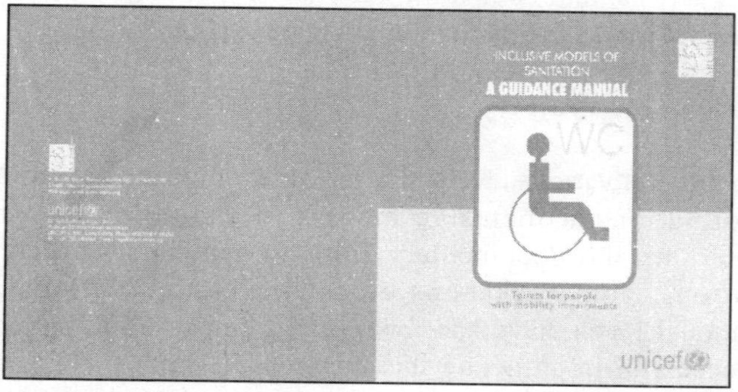

Fig. 3.10: Guidance Manual

Fig. 3.11: Low Cost Design Option

(b) Basics for wheelchair movement in Water Closet (WC) Cubicle.
(c) Entrance, door, alarm bell, signage and grab rails.
(d) Low cost alternatives.
(e) Specific issues related to household and school toilets in both rural and urban areas.

Training of Masons: Training for masons in construction of disabled friendly toilets was organized at the WATSAN Park, Bhopal and at different districts. It focused on sensitizing the masons to the needs of PWDs, and comparing the inclusive models of sanitation with general models of sanitation at the park (Fig. 3.12).

Outcome of the Project

Interventions at various levels, sharing of learning and dissemination of information on inclusive models of sanitation by way of presentations and documentary films in seminars, conferences, exhibitions, and workshops etc. at the State, National, and International levels have had far reaching impact. The project has been successful in attracting the attention of various stakeholders. As a result, several government departments/agencies have realized

Fig. 3.12: Training of Masons

the need for inclusive sanitation and have approached Arushi and UNICEF to share their expertise. The demand for such intervention is expected to grow as policy level changes are brought about. This intervention is one of its kinds in the country and with the present status of outcomes; it is expected to bear a greater impact in the future. Some outcomes are as under:

(a) Board of Secondary Education Madhya Pradesh has made it mandatory for all schools seeking recognition to have disabled friendly toilets, accessible drinking water facility and ramps.
(b) Rajya Shiksha Kendra, State government's apex academic body for school education, has issued orders for construction of disabled friendly toilets for all the upcoming school buildings.
(c) DFTs have been constructed in schools, anganwadis, and at prominent public places in 8 districts of Madhya Pradesh as models for wider replication.
(d) To consolidate the work and to generate awareness, UNICEF and Arushi have produced a video documentary and guidance manual which have been distributed in all districts of Madhya

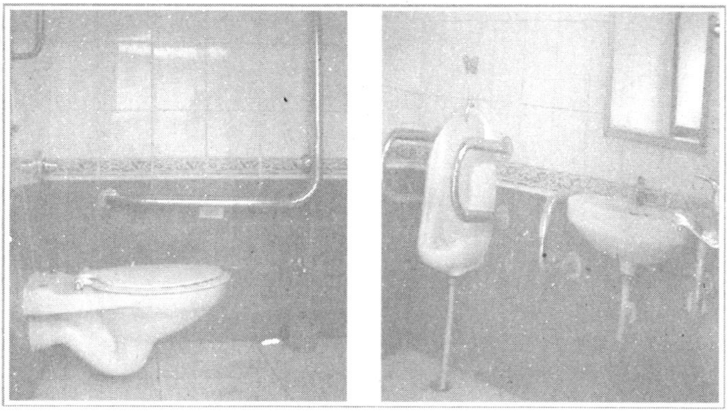

Fig. 3.13: Sanitation Models

Pradesh and to different stakeholders at national and international forums.

(e) The Government of India (GOI) has expressed interest in including the designs in the Total Sanitation Campaign (TSC) (Fig. 3.13).

(f) At the International level, experiences were shared at the 32nd WEDC Conference held in Sri Lanka in November 2006.

(g) Exhibition and presentation on the theme was made during the Prime Minister's conference at New Delhi in July 2007.

REFERENCES

1. Jones, H.E. and Reed, R.A. (2005), *Water and Sanitation for disabled people and other vulnerable groups, designing services to improve accessibility.* WEDC, Loughborough University: UK.
2. Government of India (The Persons with Disabilities (Equal Opportunities, Protection of Rights and Full Participation) Act.
3. UNICEF and Arushi (2006), Designing Disabled Friendly Sanitation-guidance manual for construction from Madhya Pradesh, India.
4. *Reviewed paper* 32nd WEDC International Conference, Colombo, Sri Lanka, 2006 sustainable development of water resources, water supply and *environmental sanitation.* A Project to Develop Inclusive Models of Sanitation for Persons with Disabilities Mr. Manu Sinha, Dr. Rohit Trivedi and Dr. Samuel Godfrey, India.

4

Production Centres-cum-Sanitary Marts

An Alternate Delivery Mechanism for Sanitation Promotion in West Bengal

Chandi Charan Dey and *Kumar Alok*

Introduction

Total Sanitation Campaign (TSC) launched by the Government of India focuses on demand generation for sanitation facilities through intensive Information, Education and Communication Campaign (IEC) activities. It is not enough just to generate demand for sanitation facilities, but also to have an effective supply chain mechanism in place that can cater to the increased demand by providing the necessary hardware and ancillary services. Thus, TSC guidelines provide for funding support for setting up of Rural Sanitary Marts and Production Centres at Block or below level for manufacturing sanitary hardware components, supply of components and skilled manpower to feed the growing demand for construction of sanitation facilities. NGOs with suitable experience of working with Panchayats are eligible to receive such funding. In addition, SHGs, Panchayats etc. are also eligible to set up such supply chain in a particular area. The RSM is typically a retail outlet that sales hardware, i.e. pans and traps, pit lining materials like rings, doors, materials for toilet superstructure and roof etc. Water filter, long handled ladles for drinking water pots, brooms, brushes and other items related to sanitation and personal hygiene are also sold. RSM is expected to provide necessary skilled manpower support and services to motivated households for setting up as well as maintaining toilets etc.

Concept of Production Centre-cum-Sanitary Mart

The concept of Production Centres and Rural Sanitary Marts was first conceived and tried in 1990 in the Intensive Sanitation Project (ISP) implemented in Medinipur district of West Bengal. The project was implemented by the Ramakrishna Mission Lokshiksha Parishad (RKMLP), Narendrapur and UNICEF in collaboration with the West Bengal Government and Medinipur Zilla Parishad. Production Centre-cum-Sanitary Marts (PC-SMs) were established with the financial support of UNICEF. 15 Cluster Organizations[1] of RKMLP were managing the PC-SM at the block level. All 15 Cluster Organisations were separately registered under the West Bengal Society (Non-profit) Registration Act, 1961 and they have democratic management system. About 1,100 village youth clubs were directly attached with these PC-SMs as village level service units. The youth clubs, according to their geographical locations, were affiliated to the respective Cluster Organizations and were entrusted to propagate the sanitation programme at the grassroots level.

West Bengal Model

Seeing the efficacy and effective service delivery abilities of the PC-SMs of Medinipur ISP, Government of West Bengal replicated this model in other districts of West Bengal with the support of UNICEF. During 1992-93, this model was replicated in 14 blocks of West Bengal. Afterwards gradually this was extended to all other blocks of the State.

In West Bengal PC-SMs are located at the block level. Each PC-SM has a sales counter and a Production Centre, where sanitary wares are manufactured. Normally there is one Production Centre-cum-Sanitary Mart per block in West Bengal but if situation demands the organisation operating the sanitary mart opens satellite PCs in different places of the block. These PC-SMs produce mosaic pans and traps, RCC squatting platforms and pit-covers etc. Each PC-SM had been provided Rs. 2,49,700 as grant from the UNICEF before introduction of TSC (presently from the TSC project) for setting up of production facility and initiate production and supply system. Generally, this grant is given to the PC-SM operating organisation in three separate installments. Detailed break up of the fund is given below in Table 4.1;

Table 4.1: Breakup of Fund for Setting up of PC-SM

Purpose/activity	*Amount in Rs.*
Construction of work shed and water vat etc.	72,000.00
Procurement of different moulds for production of sanitary components like squatting plate, mosaic pan, traps, pit cover etc.	6,000.00
Marketing support including hiring of space for showroom, sign board etc.	9,200.00
Training of village masons and motivators attached with the Sanitary Mart	12,000.00
Initial advocacy and awareness generation on sanitation	13,000.00
Revolving fund for procurement of raw materials/finished goods	1,01,500.00
Honorarium of two Mart managers for initial two years	36,000.00
Total	**2,49,700.00**

Government is providing financial support of Rs. 2,49,700[2] to the PC-SM operating organisations for development of a permanent type of supply chain system for a block. It is estimated that the PC-SM provide direct support for installation of about 25,000 toilet units in one block area. So Government's investment for establishing supply chain is around Rs. 10 per toilet unit. The supply chain system is not only supplying the hardware and installing the toilets but also supporting the PRI bodies in demand generation and sanitation advocacy in the block area. The PC-SM is to continue its services beyond the TSC project period. West Bengal has identified lowest cost unlined direct pit toilet model as the model to be universalized in TSC in the initial phase with the presumption that it would require upgradation after 3-4 years. Technical and skilled manpower support is needed for upgrading the toilet units. The PC-SM provides these supports as per the technical guidelines of the State Government. The network of PC-SM is also used for Water Quality Monitoring and Surveillance activities in West Bengal. PC-SM operating organisations are running water testing Labs, providing the surveillance services as per the demand of the Gram Panchayats, producing and marketing Iron, Arsenic and Fluoride removal filters etc.

Each PC-SM is expected to become sustainable over a period of two years time. The average cost of mosaic pan and trap is Rs. 75. The entire set of squatting plate with mosaic pan and trap fitted inside costs Rs. 490 in West Bengal and its sale price including the cost of carrying from PC to village and digging of pit and installation (Rs. 120), service charge (Rs. 40—Rs. 20 as motivator's incentive and Rs. 20 for meeting sanitary mart's overheads) etc. is presently Rs. 650 in West Bengal.

The PC-SM is staffed by two mart managers and has a network of motivators located at the Gram Sansad (Ward) level. One motivator is selected and trained for each Gram Sansad covering 200-250 families. 3-5 head masons with a group of 10-12 village masons are directly attached with the sanitary mart. A large number of women masons have been engaged by the PC-SMs in West Bengal. The production of sanitary wares has also been linked to income generation by these women masons. The PC-SM managers are paid a monthly honorarium of Rs. 1500 to Rs. 2000 other than their travel and incidental expenses. If the Managers of Sanitary Mart can sell more than 2,500 units in a single financial year, each manager is entitled to get an incentive at the rate of Rs. 5 per additional toilet above 2500 units.

Network of Motivators

Strength of sanitary marts in West Bengal lies in a strong Network of trained motivators. There is one motivator per 200-250 families. Motivators are selected jointly by the concerned Gram Panchayats and PC-SM operating organisations. Motivators are selected from the locality. A 3-day residential training programme is organised for the motivators and subsequently in-service training is also organised from time to time to keep them updated about the latest developments. Motivators are considered as grassroots level contact persons of the PC-SM who are the bridge between demand generation and supply chain. PC-SM operating organisations also keep regular contact with the Motivators, because they are the key instruments for sustainability of the PC-SM.

Motivators get an incentive of Rs. 50 per toilet for motivating the families and also supporting installation of the toilet. This incentive is paid in two installments. Service charge of Rs. 20 for motivator is built into the cost of the toilet and rest Rs. 30 is paid from IEC fund of TSC for promoting sanitation and hygiene. The wages of the masons is also built into the cost of the items produced by Production Centres.

PC-SM Promoting a Range of Toilet Models

The PC-SMs in West Bengal are not only promoting the basic toilet models but also promoting six different toilet models costing from Rs. 650 to 10,000. Families select the toilet models as per their economic affordability. The PC-SMs are also providing materials as well as technical and skilled manpower support to the households for upgradation of basic toilet models installed by the families initially (Fig. 4.1).

Process of Getting a Toilet

The motivators are instrumental in implementing the sanitation

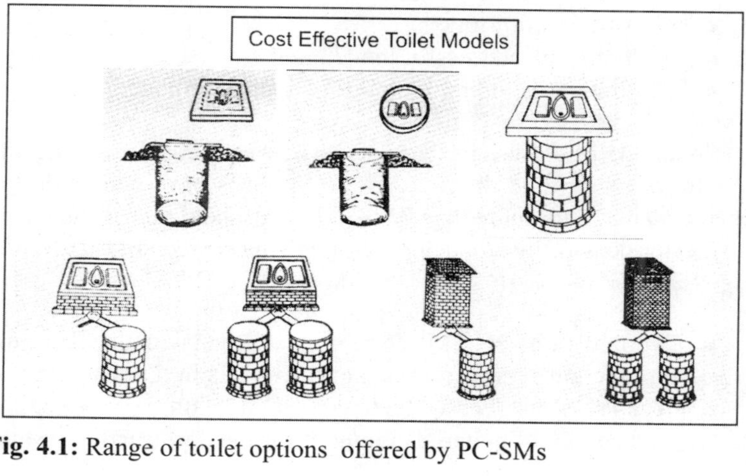

Fig. 4.1: Range of toilet options offered by PC-SMs

programme and identifying the households without toilets. When a BPL household agrees to have a toilet, it makes an advance payment of Rs. 300[3] and in case of APL household full payment of the cost of the toilet selected is advanced to the concerned motivator. Subsequently, within 15-20 days, the necessary hardware items are delivered to the household and a trained mason does the toilet installation including digging of the pit. A BPL family is given the backended incentive (subsidy) of Rs. 220 (presently) which is paid directly to the PC-SM by the BDO office on receipt of the claim including a completion report. After getting the report of toilet construction at the household level through the motivators, PC-SM submits the subsidy claim to the BDO with the certificate of toilet installation obtained from the family and the Pradhan of the concerned Gram Panchayat.

One PC-SM in One Block

In West Bengal the PC-SM are acting as the Block level machinery for delivery of TSC 'software' as well as 'hardware' in the Block area. Its activities are broadly classified as:

- Demand Generation,
- Training of masons and motivators,
- Production and procurement of hardware Components,
- Construction of toilets,
- Demonstrate successful model, and
- Follow-up including monitoring and surveillance.

So far 341 PC-SMs have been set up in West Bengal covering all the Blocks of 18 rural districts. These PC-SMs have been able to generate demand for more than 75,00,000 household toilets and have also met the demand by producing and supplying the required hardware (Fig. 4.2).

- Normally one PC-SM has been established with one or more production centres for each of the blocks in the State.
- The PC-SM serves as the outlet dealing with the production and supply of materials required for the construction of the

Fig. 4.2: Production Centre-cum-Sanitary Marts in Action (PC-SM)

sanitary facilities on the basis of demand generated through IEC activities undertaken jointly by the PC-SM itself in collaboration with the PRIs and other agencies involved in the programme.

- A PC-SM also acts as a marketing outlet for items and accessories for environmental cleanliness, personal hygiene and water quality surveillance.
- The unit runs on a 'no profit no loss' basis and operated mostly by the NGOs in West Bengal.

Government of West Bengal has formulated the specific policy guidelines for establishment and operation of PC-SM in West Bengal. Selection Process of NGOs/agencies responsible for operating PC-SMs has also been framed and circulated to all concerned. All the PC-SM operating agencies are selected following the below mentioned criteria:

Criteria for Selection of NGO/Agency for Establishing PC-SM

- Should be a non-political non-profiteering body registered under the relevant law.
- PC-SM required to be run on a "no-profit no-loss basis" catering to all sections of the rural population in need of its services.
- Should have a permanent infrastructure and access to the community concerned and must have a local base
- To have some assets and sufficient land for establishment of PC-SM.
- Should practice democratic process in managing the organisation.
- Should observe transparency in managing accounts and subjected to regular audit by qualified CA.
- The agency should not be sectarian in outlook.
- Should possess some experience in development programme implementation.
- Should have good track record of working for rural people and should be acceptable to the community it is going to work for.

Role and Responsibilities of Mart Managers

A Mart Manager is the most important functionary in the day-to-day management of the PC-SM. A PC-SM has two Mart Managers, one for Office management and the other for supervision and coordination of the field activities of the Sanitary Mart. There is no water-tight demarcation of the duties among the two managers. One of the Mart Managers of the PC-SM attends all the Review and Action Plan meetings in Block Office/Zilla Parishad etc.

The Office Manager mainly maintains accounts/records, attends to visitors, supervises the activities of masons, arranges for procurement and supply of materials to the masons, ensures quality of products, prepares reports, subsidy claim bills, utilization certificate of funds received etc. If the PC-SM runs a marketing outlet for various items for household and institutional sanitation besides the latrine components, the Office Manager also functions as in-charge of the showroom.

The Field Manager visits households with team for motivation, attends meetings, awareness camps, maintains liaison with Block, PRIs, Schools, Anganwadis etc, supervises supply and installation of toilets at household level, provides post-installation service, follows up for subsidy reimbursement etc.

In short, they play the roles of Manager/Coordinator/Liaison Officer. They are expected to provide the link between the PC-SM and the PRIs, the Nodal Department, other stakeholders, households and the institutions involved. On behalf of the PC-SM operating Organisation, the Mart Managers prepare a calendar of activities in every month and for the whole year. Basic role and functions of the Mart Managers are as follows:

- Keep records/registers/accounts of the PC-SM.
- Ensure timely procurement of materials from the market and supply to the masons so that production is not hampered.
- Keep NGO head informed about the progress/problem of work.
- Inform NGO head about decision of the meetings and Government Orders.
- Help PRI/Block in planning and organising awareness programme and HRD programme.
- Share performance with the PRI/Block every month.
- Coordinate between Nodal Department and key stakeholders.
- Suggest actions required for motivation and sustainability of programme.
- Extend service to households, Schools, anganwadis.
- Encourage community for adopting SLWM activities.
- Motivate households for construction of rainwater harvesting structure.
- Extend all possible help to PRI/Nodal Department to achieve NGP.
- Actively involve in programme for sustainability of NGP status.

Support from the Government for Strengthening the PC-SM Network

Government of West Bengal has taken adequate actions for

establishing and sustaining the PC-SM network in the State for promotion of TSC. Other than the financial support in the form of grant for establishing the PC-SM, the Government of West Bengal is putting special emphasis on Capacity Development of the PC-SM operating organisations and managers. After selection of PC-SM operating organization, a 5-day orientation on Sanitation is organised for the key functionaries of the organisations. Through this programme all the PC-SM operating organisations' heads are oriented about the programmes, working methodology, role of different stakeholders and especially the role and functions expected from the PC-SM operating organisations. Similarly a separate orientation programme is organized for the PC-SM Managers and Master Masons. Time to time re-orientation and refresher courses are also organized for the operators and managers of PC-SM. All these programmes are organised by the CCDU or by its associated organisations. Government has developed the technical drawings and designs including material and cost estimates spelt out in both engineering and non-engineering terminologies which are distributed to all the PC-SM operating organisations. Government is also providing the production manual for the masons and field functionaries of PC-SM. Regular monitoring of the quality of the PC-SM products are done involving the TSC Officials. The Government is also providing strong policy support for successful operation of PC-SM in the State. On the basis of day-to-day functioning of the PC-SM, Government formulates guidelines periodically and circulates among all concerned for smooth and effective functioning of the PC-SMs. Government has introduced a regular supervision and monitoring mechanism from the District and State Sanitation cells to identify the strengths and challenges of the PC-SM network. Monitoring is conducted at district and PC-SM level by the District and State Sanitation Officials.

Strong PC-SM Network is one of the Key Instruments for Success of TSC Movement in West Bengal

The experiment in West Bengal has been found to be very successful and accordingly adopted by the Government of India in its Total Sanitation campaign (TSC). Presently, PC-SMs of West Bengal have started manufacturing Iron and Arsenic Removal Domestic Filters, which is a very good step towards ensuring water safety at household level. More than 100 PC-SMs are involved in production and social marketing of iron and arsenic removal domestic filters in arsenic affected blocks of West Bengal. More than 80,000 units of Iron and Arsenic removal domestic filters and about 100,000 Iron removal filters have been produced and sold by the PC-SMs so far. There is an increased demand for the filters in the Iron, Arsenic and Fluoride affected areas.

PC-SM infrastructures are also being used for establishing Water Testing Laboratories in the State. So far 86 Water Testing Labs are established by the PC-SM operating NGOs in collaboration with UNICEF, Public Health Engineering Department and Panchayat and Rural Development Department, Government of West Bengal. More than 1,35,000 spot drinking water sources are also tested through 20 Labs run by the Sanitary Mart operating NGOs in arsenic affected districts. Similarly, general water quality of 3,40,000 drinking water sources have been tested through 86 Labs run by the NGO operating PC-SMs in West Bengal till September 2010.

Government of West Bengal has a plan to upgrade the PC-SM network to Public Health Mart, where almost all the services related to Public Health concern will be available round the year.

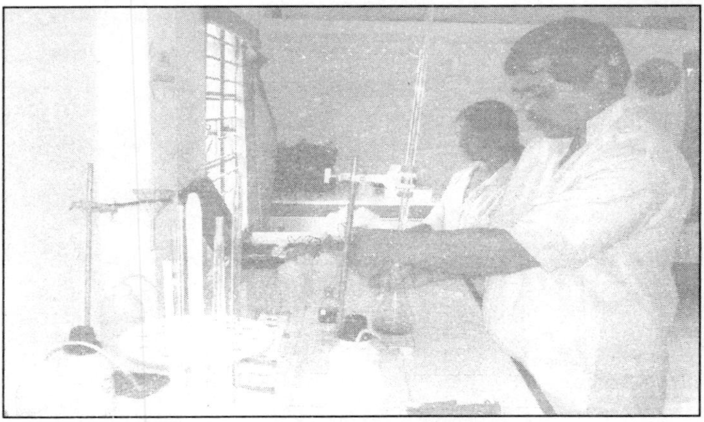

Fig. 4.3: Water Testing Lab Run by PC Operating NGO

NOTES

1. Cluster Organizations are Federations of Village Youth Clubs.
2. Even though there was a provision of providing up to Rs. 3.5 lakh per PC/RSM in TSC guidelines, Government of West Bengal continued with the earlier scheme of providing Rs. 2.49 lakh per PC-SM.
3. Presently, it is Rs. 300 in case of BPL families for the basic model, however, it used to be less earlier.

5

Integrated and Sustainable Solid and Liquid Waste Management

Vellore Model

C. Srinivasan

Introduction

It is well known that the Indus Valley Civilization had one of the most advanced and planned sanitation systems in the world. The concept of recycling is ingrained in the Indian consciousness. Since waste was just organic, it was usually dumped in a large compost pit dug in the backyard of the house and recycled locally. This practice is still prevalent in many rural societies. Many ladies still religiously collect and preserve old clothes and exchange them for new utensils, and preserve packaging material for further use.

In twentieth century India, town municipalities came into existence, who were primarily responsible for sanitation. Waste was largely organic (with a few pieces of metal, paper and cloth) and collected in bullock carts. Large trenches were dug in the compost yards outside the towns, where the waste was composted using night soil, which was also collected in bullock carts. The rich compost was sold to farmers to be used in agriculture.

What is Waste?

Waste is any material that is thrown away as unwanted. It has other names like garbage, trash and rubbish. What is considered waste by one society may not be considered so by another. For example, in societies like the US, a good quality plastic cup may be thrown away as waste. The same cup may be reused several times in India.

How does Nature Manage Its Waste?

In nature, there is no such thing as waste. What is given out by one system is taken in by another. When a tree sheds its leaves, they fall on the ground, get consumed and broken down by soil organisms into simple nutrients. The tree absorbs these nutrients once again to grow new leaves.

We will explain a systematic methodology that can be applied on a large scale involving different stakeholders to achieve 100 per cent Waste Management leaving Zero Waste. This methodology is termed as Zero Waste Management (ZWM).

Zero Waste Management (ZWM)

Our current linear resource flow uses huge amounts of raw materials and generates huge amounts of waste. This will lead our society to resource depletion. ZWM is about redesigning this resource flow so that most of what is generated as waste can be reused as raw material for further production. This resource flow is more sustainable and will take us closer to 'zero waste' to be disposed of. ZWM involves actions both before and after production.

Pre-Production Actions

Reducing Production (consumption): Producing and consuming only as much as needed will lead to reduction in waste generation.

Redesigning Production processes: Production using cleaner processes and packaging using less material, needs to be encouraged.

Production of safe and recyclable materials: It involves avoiding the use of toxic and non–recyclable materials, so that maximum resource can be recovered with least harm to the environment.

Post-Production Actions

Reuse: What is produced should be reused as many, times as possible. eg. bottles, containers, bags, etc.

Recycle: Recycling those materials that cannot be reused,. eg. Organic waste into compost, PET bottles into polyester fibres, glass bottles into glass panes, cotton rags into paper, etc.

Zero Waste Management in Vellore

Vellore area is covered around mountains and hillocks and is situated in North Tamil Nadu. We have introduced ZWM project to provide alternative environ-friendly jobs to people, who are dependent on hills for their day-to-day survival. UNICEF, DRDA, Municipalities in Vellore supported the initial projects and many private institutions and Government office campuses have also started ZWM under "Campus Maintenance and Beautification Project".

ZWM is carried out through women and men self-help groups (SHGs) after sufficient training. One supervisor, three workers and one tricycle are employed for every 250-275 families. Segregated waste (into organic and inorganic) is collected in a compartmentalized tricycle cart. The collected waste is transported to the 'Zero Waste Centre' of that municipality ward/village panchayat. Avoiding usage of very big machineries (motorized vehicles and other equipment) in ZWM processes helps to generate more employment, saves fuel and hence costs, and protects the environment from pollution. We have tried to use renewable sources of energy, local and natural (biodegradable) materials wherever possible.

Involving SHGs in ZWM

SHGs consisting of women, who are more patient and reliable are better suited to communicate with women, who are in charge of waste disposal in most households in India. Women's incomes are usually supplementary to their family incomes making their involvement in ZWM projects viable. The Government gives loans and subsidies to these groups. SHGs have an agreed code of conduct, and no team member can leave as she pleases. The SHG itself expels any member in case the code of conduct is not followed. SHG members are often local people from the neighbourhood; this encourages them to be more involved in the project. Their involvement also increases the sense of ownership of other residents in the neighbourhood.

We have started ZWM in CMC Hospital and College campus jointly with CMC administrition on 1st April, 2005 with following objectives:

- To keep the area neat and clean.
- To achieve Sustainable Zero Waste Management.
- To demonstrate complete (100%) resource recovery from inorganic waste (through reusing, recycling etc.,) and composting of organic waste by involving Women/Men Self Help Groups.

Basic infrastructure like Land and ZWM Centre, tools and accessories for Zero Waste Management Project, Power and Water Supply etc., was arranged by Christian Medical College, Vellore. Two hundred and fifty SHG members (Grassroots level Implementing Agency) took charge after getting 15 days training through "Vellore Model".

Target Beneficiaries of this project is C.M.C. Hospital, C.M.C. (College), CHAD Hospital, Rehabilitation Institute (RHI), SCHELL Eye Hospital, CMC, Women/Men Self Help Groups (250 Members), local residents etc.

Basic Facilities/Infrastructure

Following basic facilities have been created for ZWM project:

- Waste Segregation Unit.
- Recycling waste tertiary segregation and temporary storage unit.
- Vermi-composting, vermi-wash and vermi-culture unit.
- Organic waste composting unit with 36 eco-friendly aerobic composting tanks.
- Cattle shed with 28 male calves/dry cows.
- Tools storage unit.
- Workers Dinning/Meeting hall and Kitchen.
- Toilet/Urinal/Bath Room (Both for Physically Handicapped and Normal persons).
- Security/Attendant Room with Main Gate.
- Re. 1/coin phone with STD facility.

- Mega Bio-gas plants attached with filtering system (20 cum + 3 cum).
- Drying plot.
- Tools, Materials and Barrels washing place.
- Hygienic cool drinking water.
- Washing and processing units for plastic covers (Food packing covers), plastic tumblers, egg shells, citric fruits, coconut shells etc.
- Compost sieving and organic waste processing unit.
- Black plastic covers hanging unit (Drying Place).

Survey

To start the process, it is important to conduct a quick survey to assess the total number of households, commercial establishments etc. which helps in planning for waste collection and management. The survey helps in assessing the type of waste to be handled and also the total requirement of tricycles and manpower to be deployed for collecting waste. For this purpose data in simple formats was collected both for residential and commercial establishments.

1. Format for Residential Establishments

Ward No. .... Street Name .... District Name ....
Ward Member Name ....

S. No.	Head of the Family Name	Door No.	Rented (R)/Own House (O)/Empty Plot (E)	Remarks

This helps determine the number of tricycles needed for the area (one for every 250 to 275 households) and the routes they should take.

2. Format for Commercial Establishments

S. No.	Name/type of shop	Address	Ward No.

This helps determine the amount of different types of waste generated in the area. This information is important as the different types of waste need to be handled differently, e.g. Temples (flowers), clinics (syringes), barber shops (hair), tea stalls (tea dust) etc.

Awareness and Regular Updates

For success of ZWM projects it is essential that all key elements of the project are properly explained to all the households and other stakeholders so that proper segregation of waste takes place at household level itself. With greater cooperation of people, the success rate increases. For this purpose, awareness creating meetings were conducted with people at different levels who were informed about the process of segregation at household level, the difference between biodegradable and non-biodegradable waste as well as key points to remember in the form of general instructions before launching ZWM project.

List of Biodegradable and Non-Biodegradable Wastes

Biogradable	*Non-biogradable*
▪ Vegetables and fruit waste, banana leaves, coconut shell, egg shells, dry flowers ▪ Garden leaves and small twigs ▪ Non-vegetarian waste (animal bones, prawn skin, crab shell, chicken waste) ▪ Left over food, kitchen waste ▪ Dead lizards and cockroaches ▪ Ash, charcoal ▪ Coir broom ▪ Tea, coffee, floor dust ▪ House sweepings, soiled paper, finger nails and hair etc.	▪ Paper: notebooks, books, magazines, newspapers, cardboard ▪ Plastic: broken articles, water covers, milk covers, oil covers, carry bags, mineral water bottles, chocolate wrappers, paste tubes ▪ Metal: aluminium foils, iron pieces, copper, steel, tablet covers ▪ Glass: bottles, broken pieces ▪ Wood, cloth ▪ Leather: torn slippers and bags ▪ Rubber: slippers ▪ Electric wires, powerless batteries, fused bulbs and tube lights, electronic waste

General Instructions

The residents were given the following general instructions for proper implementation of ZWM project:

- Servants/maids handling waste disposal need to be trained.
- All residents need to become members of the residents welfare association in locality.
- If anyone feels uncomfortable with the worker's behaviours, that needs to be informed.
- Waste should not be littered or burnt.
- Do not throw garbage onto empty plots and drains.
- Give the project people constructive feedback on the programme.
- Do not call the workers for personal work during their work time. Residents may employ them outside working hours and pay them appropriately for their extra work.
- Inform us in advance when you plan a family function/get–together. We will arrange for a special collection from your doorstep.
- Please pack sanitary napkins using paper (not plastic) and tie it with a cotton string, and deposit it in the red bin.
- Please pack non-vegetarian waste using thick paper (not plastic) and deposit it into the green bin.
- Bring your two wastebaskets, immediately after you hear the bell ring in the morning.
- If there are large volumes of garden waste or big items like mattress, broken furniture, etc. for disposal, inform us during the morning collection. We will come again in the afternoon with an empty tricycle to collect your waste.
- If you have construction debris, inform the panchayat/municipality to collect it from your house. Do not throw it (even temporarily) onto the roadside.
- If for some reason, the tricycle does not come in the morning, please don't throw it on the road and store your waste inside till it comes the next day.
- If there are dead animals in your vicinity, inform us.
- If you cannot be at home when the tricycle arrives, keep the waste bin in a safe place, where no animal can reach and inform the workers.

Activities to be undertaken

This project targets collecting Municipal waste (Black cover) from C.M.C. Hospital, C.M.C. (College), CHAD Hospital, Rehabilitation Institute (RHI), SCHELL Eye Hospital, residential quarters area, Messes, Canteens, wards etc. So, first of all we created awareness among the residents, maids, shopkeepers, workers or labours in shops about difference in organic and inorganic waste, source segregation, current Waste Management in our street etc. To make the source segregation more effective, minimum 2 Waste Collection bins to every residents were provided. They were informed that garbage would be collected in less then 24 hours time from each and every residents including Sundays and Holidays through tricycles, by the Women Self Help Group Members and the waste would be sent to the Zero Waste Management Centre for further processing. Altogether approximately 8 tonnes of waste is collected per day from various locations in CMC hospital and transported to the ZWM centers.

Methodology

Source segregated waste (organic and inorganic) from residential areas, wards, canteens, messes etc. are brought to composting shed by the Self Help Group Members and Inorganic waste is further segregated and packed separately and sold locally. All the waste collected from the target area are further segregated. In the secondary segregation unit, wet waste is segregated into 20 items, dry waste in 17 items and food waste in 8 items. Through tertiary segregation again inorganic waste are segregated into 133 recyclable items and 10 non-recyclables. Once in a week recyclable waste are sold to local shops. Organic waste is treated in two stages, namely,

- Cattle dung Microbial decomposting, and
- Vermi-composting to produce rich organic manure.

The organic waste is laid on Composting tanks in different layers. Each layer being treated with cattle dung microbial inoculums and covered with polythene sheets. This process takes 45–60 days to complete. Separate provision will be made for non-vegetarian waste.

This cattle dung composting will increase the temperature and also reduce the volume and original weight below 50 per cent. At the end of the process the whole manure are sieved, stored and sold which can be used for Kitchen/Vegetable Roof Garden on our terrace. Cattle eatable items can be fed to 28 male calves or dry cows in the Cattle Shed. Through this process waste is converted into dung in less than 24 hours time and the same dung is fed to Bio–gas plants to trap Methane gas and the slurry is used for vermi–composting process to get best Organic Manure.

Interconnection and Interdependence: The Key to the "Vellore Model" of Integrated and Sustainable Zero Waste Management

In a natural ecosystem, e.g. a lake, there is an interconnection and interdependence between the various components—the water, soil, air, sun, microorganisms, fungi, plants, insects, fishes, birds and other life forms. Each component plays a unique role which maintains the ecosystem in balance and gives it stability and sustainability. Akin to a natural ecosystem, the "Vellore Model" of Zero Waste Management (ZWM) has nine different individual processes, which are interconnected and interdependent and which lead to "zero waste" in the end. The interconnection provides maximized efficiency and also sustainability—both economic and environmental sustainability.

The nine different processes or units are separate and well defined. However, the inputs and outputs of the nine units are closely linked to each other. When all the units are considered together, the only input to the whole system is "undesirable" waste and the outputs are useful products. Individual processes or units are shown in circles in Fig. 5.1. A circle is colour coded according to the desirability of the waste or product associated with the process. The dark red colour represents most undesirable, while the dark green represents most desirable. The amber and lighter shades of red and green represent intermediate products. The process in the white circle, represents federation activities like accounting, provides support to the rest of the processes and is in turn dependent on them.

An individual unit has its own sub-processes and operates on its own fixed time schedule. For example, the waste collection is done everyday, while aerobic composting takes 35 days to create compost from organic matter. The sub-processes in a particular unit may be interlinked within the unit, e.g. in vermicomposting, the earthworms which are produced in the process are partly reintroduced in a fresh vermicompost bin to continue the process. The individual processes are designed to be user and environment friendly, and mostly use local technologies that are not energy intensive.

Figure 5.1 shows a schematic diagram of the ZWM model.

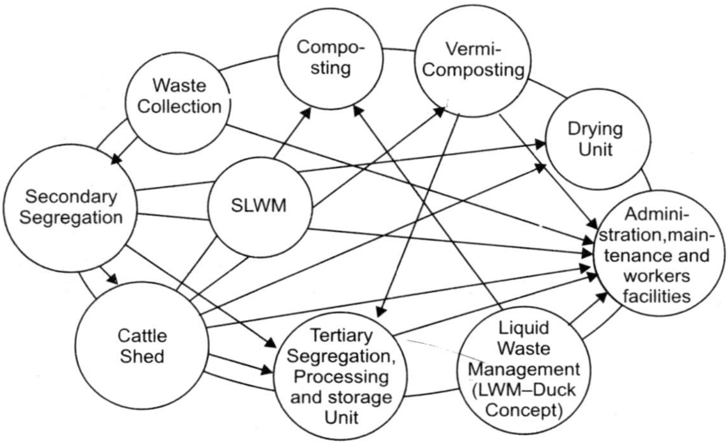

Fig. 5.1: Interconnection and Interdependence among Various Units of ZWM

From Figure 5.1, we can see the interlinking of the different units. The output of one unit is an input of one or more other units which is shown by arrows. For example, vegetable waste from the secondary segregation unit goes to the cattle shed while cow dung from the cattle shed goes to the composting, vermicomposting and drying units. We can see the systematic handling of waste from one process to another, increasing its desirability at each stage of processing.

The "Vellore model" of ZWM with separate units which work together for a common objective can be described in a nutshell as a "centralized project with decentralized processes".

Economics of ZWM

We have collected all details about the economics of a tier-3

Municipality, where waste is relocated at nearest waste dumping site and also the profit in implementing ZWM. The detailed income and expenditure involved in waste management in three different systems are compared in the subsequent sections. The three models are the existing SWM model—where the local administration manages waste collection and disposal, SHG federation model—where private contractors are involved in waste collection and disposal and the ZWM model—a partnership project managed by the community.

The existing model, where the local administration manages waste disposal-collecting, transporting and dumping waste at landfill sites. Even a small Municipality—"3rd grade/tier Municipality" in Tamil Nadu spends around Rs. 45,00,000 every year on solid waste disposal—collection and transportation alone. The details may be seen in Table 5.1[1].

Table 5.1: Cost of Waste Disposal in Existing Model

Particulars	*Monthly (Rs.)*	*Yearly (Rs.)*
Salaries		
Sanitation Officer (1)	–13,261	–1,59,132
Sanitary Inspector (1)	–9,370	–1,12,440
Field Assistant (1)	–5,500	–66,000
Sanitary Supervisors (3)	–21,000	–2,52,000
Sanitary workers (51)	–2,43,015	–29,15,904
Lorry Drivers (4)	–29,920	–3,59,040
Total	**–3,22,066**	**–38,64,516**
Equipment maintenance		
Fuel	–17,667	–2,18,000
Lorry FC	–2,000	–24,000
Lorry Insurance	–3,667	–44,000
Tubes & Tyres	–500	–6,000
Cart Maintenance	–1,000	–12,000
Cattle Fodder	–1,250	–15,000
Hay	–1,500	–18,000
Total	**–27,584**	**–3,37,000**
Miscellaneous		
Uniforms	–4,021	–48,250
Tools	–2,250	–27,000
Bleaching Powder	–4,750	–57,000
Lime	–7,800	–93,600
Phenoil	–570	–6,840
Mosquito spray	–3,667	–44,000
Total	**–23,058**	**–2,76,690**
TOTAL	**–3,72,708**	**–44,78,206**

The Vellore Model of ZWM

Following this model a "Tier-3 Municipality", implements a project in partnership with SHGs/NGOs for collecting and recycling waste which gives a yearly income of Rs. 67,000[2]. The details may be seen in Table 5.2[3].

Roles and Responsibilities in ZWM

Specific roles and responsibilities were assigned to all key stakeholders in the ZWM process. SHG members/workers were asked to conduct regular meetings among their members to solve their day-to-day problems, through their federation and it was passed as resolution and converted into Act. Salient responsibilities of the key functionaries are given on following pages.

Table 5.2: Cost/Benefit of Waste Disposal in ZWM Model

Particulars	*Monthly (Rs.)*	*Yearly (Rs.)*
Salaries		
Workers (38) @ Rs. 1,800 p.m.	–68,400	–8,20,000
Supervisors (12) @ Rs. 2,000 p.m.	–24,000	–2,88,000
Head Supervisor (1) @ Rs. 3,000 p.m.	–6,000	–72,000
Total	**–98,400**	**–11,80,800**
Equipment and other resources		
Tricycles (13) maintenance @ Rs. 300 p.m.	–3,900	–46,800
Cow Dung	–4,000	–48,000
Total	**–7,900**	**–94,800**
Others		
Medical expenses	–1,100	–13,200
Administration: Stationery, Office maintenance, communication, infrastructure	–5,000	–60,000
Total	**–6,100**	**–73,200**
Income (Minimum)		
Monthly subscription of Rs. 20 from 3,300 houses and shops	+66,000	+7,92,000
Recyclables (includes eggshell powder and coconut shells)	+12,000	+1,44,000
Compost (10 tonnes p.m. after 3 months)	+40,000	+4,80,000
Total	**+1,18,000**	**+14,16,000**
TOTAL	+6,000	+67,200

Responsibilities of Workers

1. Arrive at 7:00 a.m.
2. Take the vehicle to their area and ring the first bell at the street corner (just before entering the street). Ring it 3-4 times in a street at regular intervals. Do not ring the bell too often.

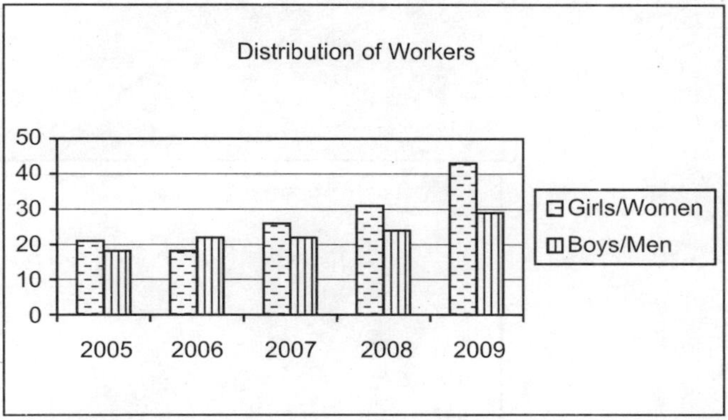

3. Collect the bins for organic and inorganic waste and deposit the contents in their respective compartments.
4. If a resident hands over un-segregated waste, try and segregate it as much as possible at the site itself.
5. If you have picked up the dustbins from a certain place in the house, put it back in the same place.
6. Do not refuse to collect waste from any household. Do not dump or burn waste along the street side or in canals. Do not sell recyclable waste yourself. If any of these get confirmed, you will be dismissed and will not be paid the month's salary.
7. Never collect money from any resident for any reason.
8. After collecting the waste, return to the ZWC.
9. After a 20–minute break for breakfast, wear mask, gloves and cap.
10. Unload the inorganic waste from the back compartment. Then remove the partition panel and unload the organic waste. Always use the rake. Never tip the vehicle to unload the waste. This may damage the vehicle.

11. Segregate cattle-eatable fresh vegetable wastes like banana leaves, beetroot leaves, cabbage leaves, greens, etc. and (if necessary) clean them by rinsing in water. Make sure it does not have any metal, plastic or glass pieces. Weigh and hand it over to the caretaker of cattle. (Find out the waste of one basket and multiply it by the number of baskets of waste.)

12. Segregate eggshells, lemon peels and coconut shells, and hand them over to the cattle caretaker.

In *Vellore*, an experiment was carried out by hanging news headlines of the day on three sides of the tricycles. This encouraged the men folk to come out with the dustbins to read the news.

13. Remove slurry from the biogas plant and mix it with water.
14. Spread out the vegetable waste (not edible by cattle) on the ground. Mix the biogas/diluted cattle dung slurry with the waste, weigh it and deposit it in the compost tank/bed currently in use. (Make sure that enough cattle slurry has been mixed with the compostable waste and that there are no plastic, metal or glass pieces left in the waste.)

15. Segregate inorganic waste into recyclable, non-recyclable and hazardous wastes.

16. Bale and pack recyclable wastes and store them in their respective areas.
17. If all this gets done earlier than 1:00 p.m., do other tasks given to you by the supervisor.
18. At 1:00 p.m., report to the supervisor in charge and leave for lunch.
19. Report back at 2:00 p.m.
20. Collect the appropriate tools from the ZWC Supervisor; enter them in the register, sign and leave for area-cleaning work with the tricycle.
21. Collect garden waste (if any household has requested earlier in the day).
22. Sweep the streets and collect organic and inorganic wastes separately.
23. Remove harmful plants like prosopis and parthenium. Adviced not to remove grass and other harmless vegetation. They help maintain soil health by keeping it covered.
24. Return at 4:30 p.m. and report to the supervisor the number of streets that were cleaned. Deposit the wastes in their respective areas in the ZWC.

Responsibilities of Field Supervisor

1. Arrive at 6:50 a.m. Mark attendance of workers and make sure that they leave for the day's work.
2. Wear gloves, mask and cap.
3. Check if workers are wearing gloves, mask and cap.
4. Check if the water bottle in the tricycle is filled with drinking water.
5. Supervise the door-to-door collection work of the workers, following the instructions given to workers.
6. Make a note of how many residents segregate and how many fail to segregate their waste. Request those who have not segregated to do so in the future.
7. Inform the residents about the availability of compost (and vermicompost if any) and make a note of those residents who would like to buy it for their gardens. Make a note of persistent defaulters and report to the Chief Supervisor.
8. Collect monthly subscription from every household at the beginning of every month and hand it over to the ZWC supervisor.
9. Make a note of the households that need to dispose of garden waste and report to the ZWC supervisor.
10. Collect complaints, suggestions and other information from the residents and report to the ZWC supervisor.
11. Report any notable incident in your area to the ZWC supervisor.
12. After collection, make sure that you return to the ZWC on time.
13. Take a 20-minute break for your breakfast.
14. Make sure that the workers wear gloves, masks and caps, and then begin to segregate the waste collected as per the requirements, and deposit in their respective storage containers/places following the instructions given to them.
15. Complete all the tricycle-related work by 1:00 p.m. Leave for lunch and return by 2:00 p.m.
16. Check if the vehicles are in good condition to be taken out for waste collection the next day.

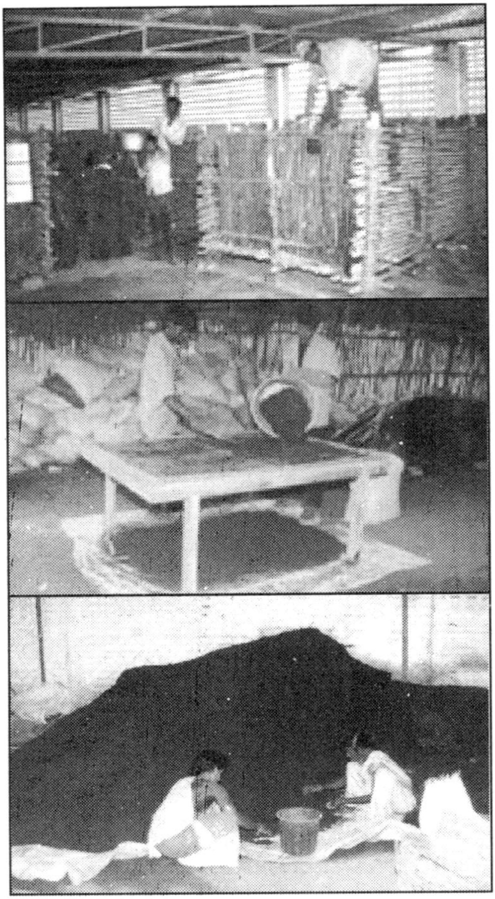

17. Harvest (remove) compost from the compost beds/tanks.
18. Sieve the compost. Pack sieved compost.
19. Moisten dried up stored compost.
20. Clean up the ZWC. Oversee the cleaning operations by the workers in their respective areas in the neighbourhood.

Responsibilities of Cattle Caretaker

1. Graze the cattle between 7:00 and 10:00 a.m.
2. Feed the cattle with the fresh organic waste separated and kept aside.

3. Clean the cattle shed floor twice everyday.
4. Clean the fodder tank once everyday.
5. Collect cattle dung at regular intervals and feed it into the biogas plant.
6. Regularly remove wash water and urine from the sump, and mix it with ragi-dal dust waste, or use it for preparing slurry.
7. Maintain the cattle clean.
8. Pound (powder) the eggshells collected on that day.
9. Clean and dry lemon peels collected during the day. Give them for grinding into powder once every month.
10. Keep the ZWC supervisor informed about how much fodder and hay is available for the cattle.
11. Keep the ZWC supervisor informed about the health of the cattle.
12. Separate the dry coconut (*copra*), the shells and fibre from the coconut waste. Give the collected *copra* for oil extraction. This oil can be used as lubricants for tricycles.
13. Maintain bio-gas plant every morning: Pour one basketful of a mixture of cattle dung and water into a 2 cc plant. Remove spent slurry from the plant to be used for composting.
14. Collect eggs laid by the hens in the ZWC.
15. During free times, do other tasks within the ZWC.

Responsibilities of ZWC Supervisor

1. Arrive by 6:50 a.m.
2. Make sure that the cattle shed is maintained as clean as possible at all times.
3. Mark attendance at different intervals.

4. Maintain daily records on the amount of organic waste collected, clean vegetable waste fed to the cattle, compost (and vermi-compost) sieved, packed and sold, eggshell powder generated and sold, lemon peel powder produced and sold, number of family functions attended to by the tricycle, number of dead animals removed, etc.
5. Make sure that the supervisors and workers carry out their assigned tasks properly.
6. Make sure that the sieved compost is kept moist at all times.
7. Collect pricelists for different types of material (glass, plastic, paper, metal.) from all the local recyclers. Compare and select the highest price for each material. Make an arrangement with each recycler to collect recyclable waste from the ZWC on a monthly basis.

A Neat and Clean Compost Shed Fit Enough for Workers to Take Breakfast

8. Record incomes from the sale of compost, eggshell powder and recyclable inorganic waste sales, and expenditures.
9. Calculate the attendance of the workers and give them salaries at the end of each month.
10. Maintain the ZWC clean at all times, especially at the end of the day when all operations for the day have been completed.

Responsibilities of Area-cleaning Supervisor

1. Make sure that streets are kept clean at all times.

2. Make sure that harmful bushes do not proliferate on empty plots.
3. Attend to calls related to clogged drains.
4. At other times, assist the ZWC supervisor in his/her work.

Incentives to the Workers

- The salaries of the workers are raised proportionately to the rise in income.
- Complete medical check up is done once in every 6 months.
- All workers are given identity cards and uniform.
- Workers who do good work are honoured every year.

Challenges Faced While Dealing with Workers

The following are the most common problems encountered with many workers:

1. They do not wash themselves clean and wear dirty clothes. This is not only unhealthy for the workers, but also creates a poor image of the workers in the minds of the residents, which then gets reflected in the way the workers get treated.
2. Giving the reason of having tea, they disappear very often and don't return for a long time during working hours. This disturbs the smooth functioning of the ZWC.
3. They arrive late, which delays the whole process thereafter, and inconveniences residents who need to leave home by 10:30 a.m.
4. Apart from one-day weekly off in a week, they take leave often disturbing the smooth functioning of the ZWC.
5. They sometimes whistle, pass comments on or speak rudely to the residents and misbehave in their presence, creating unpleasant situations.
6. They often report of puncture of tricycle tyres or some other form of repair when they need to take time off.

Advantages of ZWM—Vellore Model

Slowly ZWM has been accepted (and is being practiced) as the best solution to the problem of waste, for various reasons. Waste is segregated and resources are recovered through composting of organic waste and recycling of inorganic waste. Compost generated through ZWM is used to promote organic farming, bringing down the use of chemicals in agriculture. ZWM helps reduce the rate of virgin raw material extraction and resource depletion. ZWM minimizes waste disposal at dumpsites and reduces pollution of air, ground water and soil that result from dumping. ZWM provides income generation opportunities for the below poverty line people.

Outcome of the Project

- Everyday 8 tonnes (Minimum) of waste was collected and segregated.
- In eighteen months income through sale of recyclable waste was approximately Rs. 32,00,000.
- In eighteen months approximately Rs. 40,00,000 worth of materials was recovered from organic waste and its related products.

ZWM has proven that 'Waste' is a misplaced resource and unorganized wealth. Hence we may conclude that Waste is not Waste. We shouldn't waste money on waste but should make money from waste.

NOTES

1. This table does not indicate the social, environmental and health costs incurred because of the existing practices of solid waste disposal: transporting long distances using motorized heavy vehicles, dumping and burning etc.
2. The numbers were arrived at based on our experience in Gandhi Nagar Town Panchayat, Palavanchathu Kuppam, Vellore etc.
3. This table does not include the social, environmental and health benefits from turning waste into wealth.

6

From Sanitation to Sustainable Development

A Case Study of Mahalunge Village, Maharashtra

Megha Phansalkar

Introduction

For sustainable development, it is necessary that the seeds of initiatives are sown at the grassroots level. When the community becomes stakeholder in the development process, the results are guaranteed. With community-driven development taking the front seat, the participatory approaches have become significant. This approach involves the community as an active participant. When seeds of development are sown in the varied land, the crop yielded is also not uniform. It depends upon the level of involvement of the stakeholders. This belief has been strengthened in Mahalunge. The communities in this village have made their fallow lands into fertile plantations. The story flows from an era when no government support was available to them to an era wherein community-driven polices have come forward. The cases study brings home the fact that the people of Mahalunge with an active history of community mobilization have ensured that the new polices are harboured in fertile conditions in this village. The project work contributes in strengthening the fact that community-driven approach is the only way towards sustainable development.

Mahalunge is a village that has strengthened the belief of the government that community has to be a major stakeholder in decision making. This village, in Bhivandi block of Thane district is a rehabilitation village. For paving way for the biggest Koyana dam in Maharashtra, this village of 50 households was shifted from their homeland to Thane district. The rehabilitation policy of 1894 was brought into practice, which was not participatory in nature and hence the compensation given to the project-affected persons were meagre. The village had to struggle a lot. With no roads, no water and no electricity, no paved roads, increasing water levels and proposed windmills, the village has taken a path of self-development. In the year 2000-01, Department of Water Supply and Sanitation, Government of Maharashtra (DWSS, GoM), introduced 'Sant Gadge Baba Gram Swachhata Abhiyaan' to all villages in the state of Maharashtra. It was an open invitation to villages to participate in a competition for 'clean village'. The campaign received overwhelming response and triggered phenomenal changes in the rural Maharashtra. Sant Gadge Baba Gram Swachhata Abhiyaan provided a perfect platform for the government to put this into practice. The government took a role of a 'facilitator' in place of its previous role as a 'provider'.

Mahalunge villagers have shown that the policies, if implemented properly, can generate desired results. They are the one who have overcome all their odds and have come forward with flying colours. The village is also showing light to other villages. They have decided to make more villages like Mahalunge. Almost every second day there are visitors to this village ranging from communities to policy makers.

Campaign for Sustainable Development

Sanitation is never perceived as a priority especially in rural areas where open space is readily available even in this time of fast-growing population and rapid urbanization. Till eighties sanitation was often relegated to lower levels in priority ladder.

For the State of Maharashtra, sanitation has been an important issue. The coverage of sanitation in 2001 was only 19 per cent in the State. A thorough understanding of the situation and learning from the past experiences revealed that for an overall impact 'sanitation' should not be restricted to disposal of human excreta but should take comprehensive approach encompassing personal hygiene, home sanitation, safe water, garbage disposal, excreta disposal and wastewater disposal, and the implementation of the policy should be community led.

Taking a cue from the findings in the year 2000-01, DWSS, GoM introduced 'Sant Gadge Baba Gram Swachhata Abhiyaan' to all villages in the State of Maharashtra. The Abhiyaan offers no fund for upfront development activities; it however offers handsome prize money to villages that emerge winners, through the assessment. It was an open invitation to villages to participate in a competition for 'clean village'. The campaign received overwhelming response and triggered phenomenal changes in the rural Maharashtra. The silent and almost invisible social revolution has ignited the community spirit among village panchayats and village organizations in rural Maharashtra.

Sant Gadge Baba Gram Swachhata Abhiyaan provided a perfect platform for the government to put this into practice. Government's role as facilitator stands vindicated and a new paradigm for Community Development has emerged through the dictum: 'people initiate, government supports'. The campaign has not only cleaned the physical environment in villages but also helped to clean minds of the people in the Government and the villages. This paradigm shift yielded unprecedented results. The campaign has turned out to be the biggest IEC[1] campaign propagating environmental sanitation, personal hygiene and health measures, ever undertaken among the rural masses. This campaign has led to the mobilization of rural population to clean their houses, neighbourhoods and the entire village without much financial support from the Government. It is estimated that in response to the campaign, in its first year itself, the total investment mobilized by the communities is worth Rs. 200 crore with only Rs. 6 crore as State investment, and since year 2000 the momentum has gained strength each year. By the year 2009 up to Rs. 1000 crore have been mobilized by community efforts. Department of Water Supply and Sanitation, Government of Maharashtra, has implemented one of the most innovative programmes of community mobilization in rural Maharashtra. It gives a glimpse into the huge potential of the communities when united for a positive common cause.

The campaign by the DWSS, GoM from May 2000 prompted a competitive spirit among all the villages in the state to create a clean environment through community initiative. The village enthusiasm inspired by Sant Gadge Baba Abhiyaan and facilitated by equally motivated Government machinery, rose to hitherto unparalleled levels, to achieve the common good and well-being. In the following sections, the journey of Mahalunge village has been highlighted.

To ensure that in the Sant Gadge Baba Abhiyaan the best and cleanest villages are selected without bias and in the most transparent manner possible, committees were constituted at different levels to visit and inspect the villages and evaluate their performance. Villages are inspected at five different levels in order to be judged the 'cleanest village' in the State. In Thane, at the micro level, a Zilla Parishad[2] councillors' constituency-level committee visits all the participating villages in the constituency and selects the three best villages. These judging committees are a mix of officials and non-officials. It is ensured that no one judges a village in his own block. Also scores have to be awarded on the spot and the reasons explained. For the state-level prize, a review is done by a second team. The costs are met from local government funds, the state contributes nothing. The judges are required to consider as many as 85 criteria. The scope, the depth and the transparency are striking. Villagers acknowledge the fairness of the process. Some of the creteria for judgement are listed below, which indicate the depth of the evaluation process:

- What is the extent of popular involvement? Have the works been let to undeserving contractors and window-dressed?
- What is the state of the toilets and what is the count?
- Has the village rid itself of scavengers?
- Are non-conventional energy devices being used?
- How well are the schools kept? What is the awareness level regarding plastic's potential to degrade environment?
- How clean are the shops and eateries?
- Are irrigation and utility charges paid on time?
- How well is water managed? Are fuel efficient, and smokeless stoves in use?
- Have there been epidemics or chronic heath problems in the village?
- How well is the small family norm adhered to?

Process of Self-Development

For Mahalunge it was an opportunity knocking at their door. They decided to participate in the campaign in the first year, i.e. year 2000. In Mahalunge the competition was launched on 2nd October, a date designated for Gram Sabhas across the State. The Gram Sabha[3] was used as a launching pad for the competition. The session was facilitated by Gram-sevak[4]. In the Gram Sabha it was decided that Mahalunge would participate in this competition. Selected members made a visit to Ralegan Shindi[5] and then they decided their path of action. Subsequently more Gram Sabhas were conducted in the village, to prepare the village for participating in the campaign. Thus, we can see that the competition uses existing institutions and traditions to encourage participation without incurring any extra costs.

As per the guidelines of the campaign following key activities were initiated in the village:

- Clean-up and garbage disposal.
- Cleaning and repairing of septic tanks and sanitation works.
- Cleaning up the schools and their premises.
- Cleaning up homes and surroundings.
- Sessions on cleanliness were arranged by the Gram Panchayat to make the community aware of its roles.
- Repairs of toilets were undertaken and planning for new toilets was initiated.
- Water issues like maintaining quality, increasing the water level, watershed-management-related activities were initiated.
- Personal hygiene was focused at the school level and household level.
- *Shramdan* or physical participation to repair roads and public places were mobilized.
- Care of livestock and cleaning of their dwellings were initiated.

In the Village: The competition enthused the villagers and motivated them to undertake various activities necessary for village sanitation. An unprecedented synergy was created among villagers, its leaders and government officials, to ensure implementation of all the activities. This provided a platform for discussion followed by actions to an otherwise neglected issue of rural sanitation. The general outcomes of this initiative in the village are:

- There is a perceptible reduction in epidemics and water-related diseases in last two years.
- The mobilization of the youth, women and students is noticeable.
- Many people have remarked that this campaign has not only cleaned the physical environment in the villages, but also helped to clean minds of the people in the villages.
- The villagers, which are divided on certain issues, have been united and integrated through this programme for overall welfare of the community.
- The village has proved the slogan of the campaign "From Cleanliness to Prosperity".

The government officials provided an effective knowledge link by providing the villagers necessary information regarding available technologies for sanitation and are carrying out very effective IEC campaign in rural areas. The inter-department coordination is worth mentioning in this campaign. The villagers' enthusiasm also increased due to a desire to earn honour and they surprised officials by their readiness to help themselves. The basic facts about the village are given in Table 6.1.

Initially the village was under Group-Gram Panchayat[6]. After various representations Mahlunge was recognized as Gram Panchayat in 1995. Later in the year 1999, in order to implement the 73rd Constitutional Amendment, areas dominated by tribal population were notified as tribal belts and the villages falling under the notified area were declared for tribal reservation where the Sarpanch and one-third of the Gram Panchayat members were to be from tribal community. This village is surrounded by tribal villages, hence the surveyor or Talhati[7] by mistake marked this village as notified area reserved for tribal representation.

Ironically Mahalunge village does not have a single tribal family, so they couldn't fulfil the reservation conditions. Since 1999, they

Table 6.1: Village at a Glance

Name of the Gram Panchayat: Mahalunge			
Category	Non-tribal	No. of Mahila Mandals	01
		No. of Yuvak Mandals	04
Taluka and District	Bhivandi, Thane	No. of SHGs	06
Total Population	505	BPL Houses	17
No. of Houses	91	No. of Public Well	03
No. of Males	253	No. of Public Bore wells	01
No. of Females	252	No. of Piped Water Supply Scheme	01
Sanitation-related Data			
No. of Individual Toilets	91	No. of Compost Pits (1 pit/8 Houses)	12
No. of Community Toilets	00	No. of Paras Bags	20
No. of Soak Pits	91	No. of Smokeless Chulhas	65
Vermiculture Projects on Solid Waste	04		

do not have an elected body to take care of the Gram Panchayat affairs. As per the policy, there is 80 per cent reservation for tribal candidates and in a Gram Panchayat only 2 seats are from general category. Village doesn't have members from the tribal category. 'Prashasak'[8], normally an extension officer has been nominated by the Zilla Parishad, who runs the affairs of the village panchayat. The Zilla Parishad has also put their hands up and has said that the situation calls for amending the Constitution which was not in their hands.

This kind of arrangement has hampered the spirit of local self-governance and the community initiatives for progress. Enough representations have been made at the required levels with no relief till date. The villagers have requested the authorities to recognize them as a special case of rehabilitation project and remove them from the 'tribal notified' area. The total budget of the Gram Panchayat is quite low and the only sources of income are the water tariff and the house tax.

'Since we had nothing to lose and had not much means to earn the livelihood, and due to proximity to Thane and Mumbai, our children have been focused on their education, and at least we could offer better education to the younger generation', says Nana, the Iron man behind this movement. The village has generated engineers and doctors as well. The new generation is mostly out for jobs, and visits the village on special occasions. They have always participated in the community initiatives and have helped financially and technically whenever required. As a result the village has a hefty kitty in its hands. As part of the community initiatives, all the ladies start cleaning the village at 5 a.m. from the main gate. Similarly, once in a week, (normally Tuesday) the men gather at the temple and decide about the activities that require attention, and start taking action on them one by one.

Component-wise Progress

Making the Village Open-Defecation Free

When the village decided to participate in the 'Sant Gadge Baba Abhiyaan', the first thing that came into their mind was that the village should be 100 per cent open-defecation free. A few families had toilets but almost 60 per cent households were using the fields. The community members said that when they used to go to provide labour contribution for the Bandhara[9]. They had to first clean the area as it used to be impossible to stand due to bad odour. Now the village is proud to have individual toilets and even a small child refuses to defecate in the open. The village has used two-pit technology, to ensure that when one pit fills they don't have to go outside. The key issues they faced while achieving this target was that 50 families were BPL and hence the village decided to contribute from Panchayat's[10] fund for their toilets. They were asked to repay in due course.

There was an issue of linking the toilets to the gobar-gas plants, as the old generation was not ready to accept this technology and cook food from the gas generated from the human excreta. However, the younger generation could finally convince the community properly. Local masons were used and the villagers contributed labour. Some households went for low-cost options and are now upgrading the toilet as per their capacity. Due to collective efforts, on 20 December, 2003, the village declared itself as open-defecation-free village. The village has not promoted a single community toilet, as they realized that maintenance would become a big issue later on. The aganwadi[11] and the school have been provided with toilet and water supply. The village has also contributed from the prize money for repair of the old toilets of the school.

Excreta Management

Along with dairy units, gobar-gas units have also been taken up in the village. All the houses in the village use gobar-gas units. These units have also been attached to the toilets. The gas is used for cooking for limited hours. Total 48 units had been installed in 2003, out of which 8 have been closed as the families have moved out of the village and come only on few occasions. Forty units are working properly. In each house the wastewater is connected to the soak pit. The community members through labour contribution have made the soak pits. The remaining water is taken to the kitchen garden. Almost each house has a small or big kitchen garden, where vegetables, fruits plants are nurtured with the wastewater (Box 6.1).

Solid-Waste Disposal

Under the technical guidance provided by the Department of Water Supply and Sanitation Department and Zilla Parishad, Thane, the community members through voluntary labour constructed the community waste-disposal pit. Individual waste-disposal pits were

Box 6.1: Key Points of Excreta Management

- All the toilets were constructed by the community itself.
- Type of technology used: Two pit.
- 100 per cent private toilets for each household.
- Community toilets for visitors are proposed.
- All the toilets are connected with the bio-gas plant.
- Each toilet has been provided with water tap.
- Low-cost technology has been used for economic reasons.
- Gram Panchayat supported BPL families and provided loan so that the village could become open-defecation free as per the target.

constructed by the households with their own expenses. Vermiculture units have also been taken up by individual households.

Sepatrate waste bins for dry and wet garbage are kept at suitable locations in the village. In each house different coloured bins are kept for dry and wet garbage. The green and red coloured bins were provided by the Gram Panchayat in the year 2003 utilizing 20 per cent of the prize money meant for individual benefit. All the household garbage is separated into dry and wet garbage at household level. The community through voluntary labour has built one Nadep-type community garbage-disposal unit. The wet garbage of each household is gathered into the community-wet bin, and is then directed towards the 'Nadep Pit'.[12]

Since only 96 households reside in the village one pit of 10-feet length, 3-feet breadth and 3-feet depth is sufficient for the whole year. Every year the bio fertilizer so produced is sold to local farmers through auction. The dry garbage is also collected from each household for the Vermiculture units of the village maintained by individual villagers. Seven Vermiculture units are functional in the village. Individual households own the Vermiculture units, which are a source of income. Apart form this, many households have also made individual compost pits in their premises. This again operates as per yearly cycle, where the entire garbage is taken out before rainfall and used for the kitchen garden. Due to regular usage of organic manure the use of chemical fertilizers have been reduced (Box 6.2).

Agriculture and Social Forestry

Farming is the main occupation of the community. The total land under agriculture is 218 acres and the land holding is very small. Normally it ranges between 2–5 acres per household. With the advent

Box 6.2: Waste-water Management

- Soak pits in each house.
- Kitchen garden in each house.
- Open village drains cleaned by the women together on every Tuesday.
- Fish tank of "Gappi mase" (this fish eats mosquito eggs and help in reducing mosquitos.

of the community initiatives and increase in water levels, 30 acres of land has been brought under double cropping. This forms the belt near the river 'Shaitani'[13]. In the winter season local pulses and vegetables are grown. The organic manure produced in the village is used in the field. The community proposed to construct two farm ponds in the year 2007 to increase the water level of the area. Since the village always takes lead in mobilizing community labour, many development initiatives take place naturally in the village. For example with community labour more than 5000 trees have been planted in about 2 acres of land on the hillock of the village. The entire hill, which was barren, has been converted into a green hillock. The only problem the village faces is of shortage of water in summer months for watering the trees. This initiative has also helped in increasing the water level. In the first year, keeping aesthetics in mind Ashoka trees were planted, which requires more water. Now the community has decided to plant the tree called 'Karaj'[14] which helps to keep the air clean and also requires less water.

Community Temple

Normally each village has a community temple, which is also used for various social functions. Mahalunge, being a rehabilitated village, did not have any temple in the village. The community built a small temple in the village through its own effort and called it 'Samaj Mandir'. In 1992 the community decided to renovate it. A local architect prepared a design and it was agreed that the temple shall be renovated as per the design in 1995. An amount of Rs. 30 lakh was required for the same. The village decided that they will provide labour contribution as much as possible to save the cost. For specilised work external labourer were sought, and each household provided them food one by one, thereby reducing some costs. The money needed for buying constructiuon materials was also raised through community contributions.

The present temple made through community contribution and labour is an exemplary case study of resource mobilization. The architecture of the temple is very appealing and it has given a place for the community to gather and have meetings, discussions, training sessions, etc. Today the temple premises are even used for film shootings.

The Strategy of Self-Development

The villagers went to Raleganshindi[15] to learn how this village had been socially transformed after prohibiting certain undesirable social practices. Mahalunge also followed the same five-prohibition strategy:

- Daru Bandi (liqour prohibition)
- Nas Bandi (compulsory family planning)
- Tanta Bandi (no political groups or fights)
- Katai Bandi (prohibition of tree felling)
- Ughadi Hagandari Bandi (prohibition on open defecation)

The implementation of these prohibitions is done strictly and all villagers abide by the community decisions. The new generation has also easily acquired these good practices. For this initiative hardly any technical guidance is required but only self-discipline, determination and able leadership make it possible.

'Since we have made our village open-defecation free, there has been a remarkable reduction in the health problems. We also test the water quality regularly', says a local resident. Everyday chlorination is done. To reduce the mosquitoes in the tanks a local fish named 'Gappi-Mase' is harboured. They eat the eggs of the mosquitoes to reduce their reproduction. The soak pits and solid and liquid waste management ensures that the village is clean. Since 2003, no major disease outbreak has occurred, and the incidences of water-borne and water-related diseases has been almost nil. Even diarrhoea among children a thing of the past. The villagers say that the expenditure on health has reduced drastically. The village does not have a Primary Health Centre (PHC), hence people have no option but visiting private doctors. Prior to 2003, every year each household used to spend Rs. 4000–5000 for visiting the private doctors, which has now drastically reduced (Box 6.3).

Implementation Schedule for Sant Gadge Baba Abhiyaan

The Sant Gadge Baba Abhiyaan was implemented in the village following a structured and systematic approach. After the launch of the programme on every birth anniversary of Mahatma Gandhi a

Box 6.3: From Sanitation to Sustainable Development: Events in Chronological Order

- Year 1960: The process of rehabilitation started; the villagers knew that their homes would be submerged.
- Year 1962: Shifted from Satara to Thane, made temporary houses, started rice cultivation on the available land. No infrastructure, no drinking water in vicinity.
- Year 1972–76: Suffered major droughts, hence started community farming for survival.
- Year 1992–95: Started community dairy farming as a source of subsidiary income to the families.
- Year 2001: Participated in the Sant Gadge Baba Abhiyaan; stood second at the block level; and earned Rs. 2 lakh as prize money.
- Year 2002: Participated in the Sant Gadge Baba Abhiyaan—stood first at the block and district levels.
- Year 2003: Stood first in the division-level competition.
- Year 2004: Got Nirmal Gram Puraskar from the Government of India.
- Year 2005: Stood second at the State-level in the Sant Gadge Baba Clean Village competition. Got Dr. Ambedkar Samta Puraskar of Rs. 3 lakh.
- Year 2006: Selected from the block for the incentive fund component under the Jalswarajaya project of Department of Water Supply and Sanitation to get a sum of Rs. 10 lakh as untied fund for implementing innovative ideas.
- Year 2007: Have prepared the design of their new Gram Panchayat building, which shall house a visitor gallery, library, counselling centre for farmers and Gram Schivalaya. The Gram Panchayat office-cum-Schivalaya shall act as one-stop information centre for the people from other villages, for guidance on rural development.
- Year 2007: Other villages under the Koyana rehabilitation package got support from Mahalunge to become Nirmal Gram, resulting in Nivdi, Morni and Kusapur villages getting NGP Award in 2007.
- Year 2008: Initiated the construction of Gram Sachivalaya building, which would house library and rural development training centre, through renovation of the existing Gram Panchyat office building. This was to cost Rs. 20 lakh.
- Year 2009: Completion of the Gram Sachivalaya building and fully functioning rural development centre with multi-media facilities for presentation and other activities.

month long date-wise schedule is worked out through community consultation. Each day is assigned for a particular sanitation-related activity. The entire community including women and youth plan the day events carefully. The day-wise agenda is shown in Table 6.2.

Voluntary Labour Donated by the Community

The community has contributed a lot in the form of labour over the past many years. An analysis of the labour contributed reveals that

Table 6.2: Day-Wise Programme under Sant Gadge Baba Abhiyaan

S. No.	*Day Number*	*Activities*
1.	Day 0	Conducted Gram Sabha and decided to participate in Sant Gadge Baba Abhiyaan.
2.	Day 1 & 2	Village cleaning activities were done with community participation.
3.	Day 5 & 6	Maintenance of soaks pits and repair.
4.	Day 7 & 8	Cleanliness of school and public buildings.
5.	Day 9 & 10	Improving aesthetically the houses and their premises through competitions.
6.	Day 11 & 12	Exhibition of items related to cleanliness: of cleanly-ness in hygiene and behaviour.
7.	Day 13 & 14	Construction and repairing of toilets.
8.	Day 15 & 16	Hands-on demonstration for water-quality maintenance.
9.	Day 17 & 18	Personal hygiene awareness activities and rally.
10.	Day 19 & 20	Repair and cleanliness of roads.
11.	Day 21 & 22	Livestock maintenance and cleaning programme, and animal-health competition
12.	Day 23 & 24	Tree plantation, kitchen-garden promotion and non-conventional energy promotion through solar street-lights and gobar gas.
13.	Day 25 & 26	Slogan writing and essay writing competitions, and awareness drive against tobacco and liquor.
14.	Day 27 & 28	Healthy-baby competition and health talk show on women and child growth.
15.	Day 29 & 30	Waste-water management initiatives and cleaning of gutters.
16.	Day 31	Oath ceremony was arranged for six-pronged prohibit-tion policy.

during 2003-04, 2004-05 and 2005-06 itself the community mobilized more than 9,700 man-days resulting in a cash mobilization of approximately Rs. 6.75 lakh. This kind of contribution does not require much technical knowledge, but is a pure form of physical and unskilled labour. It needs a lot of community motivation and mobilization. Tables 6.3, 6.4 and 6.5 indicate the labour contribution during the three consecutive years.

During 2003-04, 4,936 man-days have been volunteered; the calculated cost of this volunteered labour is Rs. 3,45,520.

During 2004-05, total 3,099 man-days have been volunteered; the calculated cost of this volunteered labour is Rs. 2,17,100.

During 2005-06, total 1,730 man-days have been volunteered; the calculated cost of this volunteered labour is Rs. 1,10,100.

Table 6.3: Labour Contribution by Community during 2003-04

S. No.	*Work done through people's participation*	*Number*	*Total cost in Rs.*	*Man-days*
1.	Internal Road—50 metre	1	6,300	90
2.	Construction of Bandhara[16] on the river	5	30,380	434
3.	Road-side gap filling, cleaning of partly constructed gutters and cleaning of common building premises	1	15,680	224
4.	Extension of the play ground	1	21,840	312
5.	Road-side gap filling and cleaning common building premises	1	1,24,600	1780
6.	Community temple construction	1	63,000	900
7.	Houses painting	1	70,000	1000
8.	Construction of primary school toilets	1	4,830	69
9.	Maruti temple and community temple painting	3	1,050	15
10.	Cleaning of four wells	1	2,870	41
11.	Making 90 soak pits	90	3,150	45
12.	Nadep pits	1	700	10
13.	Seating arrangement made around two trees	2	700	10
14.	Digging pits	12	420	6
15.	Total		3,45,520	4936

Table 6.4: Labour Contribution by Community during 2004-05

S No.	Work done through people's participation	Number	Total cost in Rs.	Man-days
1.	Construction of Bandhara on the river	3	15,700	224
2.	Road-side gap filling, cleaning of partly constructed gutters and cleaning of common building premises	4	1,15,000	1642
3.	Soak pits reconstruction and maintenance	90	3,200	45
4.	Internal road—100 metre	2	7,700	110
5.	Community temple construction	1	65,000	928
6.	Schools' & latrines' sanitation and Nadep pits maintenance	2	1,200	17
7.	Security wall constructed around the school and the community temple	2	1,300	18
8.	Water tank cleaning and purification of four wells	2	2,000	29
9.	Village cleaning	1	6,000	86
	Total		**2,17,100**	**3,099**

Table 6.5: Work done by Villagers through Voluntary Labour during the year 2005-06

S. No.	Work done through people's participation	Number	Total cost in Rs.	Man-days
1.	Construction of Bandhara on the river	3	15,700	224
2.	Road-side gap filling, cleaning of partly constructed gutters and cleaning of common building premises	4	25,000	401
3.	Soak pits reconstruction and maintenance	90	3,200	45
4.	Community temple construction	1	65,000	928
5.	Schools' & latrines' sanitation and Nadep pits maintenance	2	1,200	17
6.	Water tank cleaning and purification of four wells	2	2,000	29
7.	Village cleaning	1	6,000	86
	Total		**1,10,100**	**1,730**

The Rewards

'*I learn experiences from this village to develop rural area in my country.*' S. Chanpai from Thailand

'*I love your village.*', B.C. Chegpa, Bhutan.

'*We teachers and 160 students visited your village; it is inspiring to all visitors. Cleanliness is appreciable*'. Head Master, Little Angel Primary School, Borivali, Mumbai.

...... And the list goes on. These are excerpts from the visitors' book of Mahalunge village.

'Today it seems it is a rest day, otherwise everyday we have visitors to the village', says one community member. Almost everyday there are visitors to Mahalunge. The village has seen visitors from various states as well as countries. School children also come on educational tour to the village. The most valued visitors are the community members who come from other villages. Exposure visit becomes a source of inspiration and guidance for the community members who intend to emulate the success formula of Mahalunge. Mahalunge has been able to receive a large number of awards for the exemplary community initiative, which are listed in Table 6.6.

Mahalunge village used these funds for various individual as well as community initiatives, which are listed below:

- Individual benefits given to community members to purchase

Table 6.6: The List of Awards Received by the Mahalunge Village

S. No.	*Award*	*Year*	*Amount in Rs.*	*Level*
1.	Saint Gadge Baba Village Cleanliness Prize (2nd)	2002-03	3 lakh	District
2.	Saint Gadge Baba Village Cleanliness Prize (1st)	2003-04	5 lakh	District
3.	Saint Gadge Baba Village Cleanliness Prize (1st)	2004-05	Repeat prize not given	District
4.	Saint Gadge Baba Village Cleanliness Prize (2nd)	2003-04	6 lakh	Region
5.	Saint Gadge Baba Village Cleanliness Prize (2nd). Prize money was distributed between 2 villages, as both being on second place.	2004-05	10 lakh	State
6.	Dr. Baba Saheb Ambedkar Samta Prize	2004-05	3 lakh	State
7.	Nirmal Gram Puraskar, Total Sanitation Campaign, Government of India	2004-05	2 lakh	National
8.	Selected by Department of Water Supply and Sanitation, GOM, under Incentive fund pilot project	2005-06	10 lakh	State

separate bins for dry and wet waste disposal and other related activities—Rs. 65,000.

- Repairing the building of the Gram Panchayat office—Rs. 20,000.
- Toilet repair in the school—Rs. 20,000.
- Making gutters for storm water drain—Rs. 30,000.
- Expenditure on slogan writing and generating awareness—Rs. 27,000.
- Expenditure on inter-state visitors—Rs. 22,200. Visitors from 18 countries have visited Mahalunge.
- Making shops on the road—Rs. 49,000. The shop is given on rent of Rs. 300 per month.
- Children's park—Rs. 49,900.
- 2 per cent of the prize money on celebration—Rs. 15,000.
- Expenditure on travel to other villages for exposure visits—Rs. 14,346.
- Wall around the children's park—Rs. 46,900.
- Gutter for the remaining village—Rs. 17,000.
- Mosquito repellent machine—Rs. 21,500.
- Office expense—Rs. 8,020.
- Construction of Gram Schivalaya office building—Rs. 16,73,716.
- Gram Panchayat office building repair—Rs. 40,000.

The hardship the village has experienced during the past 40 years has started bearing fruits:

- There is a perceptible reduction in epidemics and water-related diseases in the last two years.
- The mobilization of the youth, women and students is noticeable.
- The village is clean and neat.
- The sanitation drive has not only cleaned the physical environment in the village, but also helped to clean minds of the people in the village. The village, which is divided on some issues, has been united and integrated through this programme.
- The village has basic infrastructure like roads, school and electricity.

- The drinking water problem has been solved and each household has a tap connection.
- The drinking water quality is maintained and water-testing takes place regularly.
- The village is lush green due to social forestry initiatives.
- A few fields yield double crop now, the farmers are going ahead with winter crop through their power pumps.
- The small dams made out of cement bags have increased the water level.
- The waste management is helping generate income in the form of vermiculture and gas for cooking.
- The village people have purchased a computer for the school and want their kids to be in the mainstream.

There are three main factors that have helped the sustainability of the performance achieved by Mahalunge during the competition and thereafter:

- Group motivation triggered by a challenge persists if more and more challenges are put forth in front of the group. In other words a series of challenge sustains group motivation.
- Performance achieved during a group competition is sustained because the purpose of the competition is in line with the needs and wants of all individuals in the group.
- Sustainability of the group spirit depended on ability of the group to evolve mechanisms for transparent, consensus-oriented decisions during their weekly meetings and Gram Sabhas.

The community goes ahead with helping hands to a few BPL families of the village thereby ensuring that they also ride the wave of sustainability. Says Nana 'We were 1,500 people when we came here, at one time all households were under BPL category, which came to 47, then 17 and now only one family is under BPL category. The village has helped BPL families through various Gram Panchayat and other convergence scheme to reduce the poverty levels.

The Overall Impact

The impact is manifold. It demonstrated multi-faceted paradigm shift in the way government works at village level especially in sanitation sector. Following are some of the impacts of this innovation:

- The competition has changed focus of the intervention from individual to community as a whole.
- The campaign is able to leverage large community investment for a very small fiscal incentive from the government.
- The campaign does not provide any subsidy but is based on community involvement and participation. The incentive is provided in the form of cash reward. In other words, the regime of subsidies has been changed into regime of rewards.
- 'Status' is one of the important motivations behind actions. The campaign acknowledged this and evolved around ideas like community reputation and status. The campaign has induced unity amongst village communities for a common cause and provided them recognition for their efforts. The competition mode provided much sought after reputation to these communities.
- The government does not impose any technology but works as a facilitator to satisfy emerging demands put forth by the communities.
- The competition provides stimulus to all tiers of governance ranging from the State Government to the Village Panchayats. The assessment is carried out at each level of governance. Further the competition has effectively shifted the responsibility for implementation from State Government to lower tiers of government.
- The assessment and ranking is based on overall cleanliness and judicious use of resources on pre-defined list of parameters, thereby enhancing transparency in assessment.

The village community is planning to make the achievement sustainable and wants to ensure that the Gram Panchayat has enough resources. Hence, village is planning to generate resources through innovative means like selling the vacant plots for new families, extending the village boundary, promoting solar and wind energy, etc.

- Selling the vacant plots for new families: When the families settled in Mahalunge a plot of 50 by 80 sq. metres was allotted to each family. Some plots are vacant. The community has plans to sell these plots to the joint families who wish to have another house to accommodate their large families.
- Extending the village boundary: A proposal has been submitted for extension of the village boundary. This will help the village to generate some resources. The village is also looking forward to do some major interventions in the watershed development.
- With the new government resolution now the village has to bear the cost of the public light posts which is a big burden for Mahalunge. Similarly, the individual household also has to pay hefty bills. As a permanent solution to this problem the village is planning to shift to solar and wind energy. Two units of solar electricity for street lighting have already been established.

The village has been given NGO status, which means that if in any project services of an NGO are required, the village can be hired. Mahalunge has already helped other villages in rehabilitation and in eliminating the practice of open defecation. 'Today four villages have become open-defecation free, through our motivation and guidance", Nana says proudly, 'We guide the villages on technology, communication skills, atitudinal change'. After getting Nirmal Gram Puraskar from the Government of India in 2004–05, Mahalunge has formed a group of 15–20 members including women, who have volunteered to guide the other villagers on regular basis. In 2006, two villages, Uchat, Nivadi have applied for the Nirmal Gram Puraskar.

The competition triggered series of actions in many spheres. Its effects were mostly visible at the village level. At the institutional level, for the first time such a large section of government functionaries were directly involved in activities related to sanitation.

This paradigm shift yielded unprecedented results. Mahalunge is one such village that made use of the golden opportunity. From a rehabilitated village in 1962, it has become a model of rural development after bagging the Nirmal Gram Puraskar in 2005 under the Total Sanitation Campaign and now has a fully functioning Rural Development Training Centre, where trained volunteers give training through practical and theory sessions. It has shown that if the community decides and policy supports, there is nothing which can stop the sustainable progress of our villages.

NOTES

1. Information, Education and Communication.
2. Zilla Parishad is the government body at the district level, which coordinates and implements development projects within the district.
3. Gram Sabha is a forum/meeting which all adults above 18 years can attend and discuss on village related issues.
4. Gram Sevak is a government representative in the village to guide the village on development schemes.
5. Ralegan Shindi village has been developed by Shri Anna Hajare, noted social reformer and activist. It was the first model for sustainable rural development.
6. Sometimes two or more villages are clubbed together to form Group-Gram Panchayat when the population of an individual village is less than 300.
7. Block level representative of revenue department who is authorized by the local government for land related surveying, decision, etc.
8. Administrator appointed by the Zilla Panchayat.
9. Bandhara is a small dam on the river made by mud filled in cement bags through labour to stop the flowing water thereby increasing seepage and water level in the neighbouring areas.
10. Village Governing Body.
11. Aganwadi is a term used for playschools run by the government in the rural areas.
12. Nadep is a type of technology for solid-waste disposal popular in India.
13. Shaitani is name of the local river in Mahalunge.
14. Local tree which survives in less water.
15. Village of the famous social activist Shri Anna Hazare.
16. Bandhara is a small dam made through piling mud in cement bags for reducing the water flow and increasing seepage of water to the nearby lands.

7

Mahila Samakhya in Bihar

Empowering to Achieve Nirmal Gram Puraskar

Sanjay Dubey and *Jawed Alam*

During ancient times the women enjoyed equal status with that of men but the patriarchal joint-family system has lowered the status of women that is persisting even today. Bihar is home to multi caste and multi-dialect groups of eighty three million people. Bihar is now confronted with challenges in providing proper rural water supply, hygiene and sanitation facilities. The condition in terms of sanitation is quite challenging. As per the census 2011 more than 85 per cent rural households in Bihar defecate in the open. Poor sanitation has become a serious threat to public health. The women and children in particular have been the worst affected victims.

Mahila Samakhya (MS) was visualized as a unit of Bihar Education Project (BEP) to ensure a clear policy commitment to women's empowerment through education and training in the development projects.

Fig. 7.1: Kavita is proud of her toilet

Now MS is functioning as an autonomous body. MS has realized sanitation and hygiene as critical to the interest of women empowerment. Hence it took the decision to address the problem of sanitation and hygiene as an urgent development necessity.

Mahila Samakhya (MS) has been designed to fulfil the commitment of affirmative action in support of women's education mandated in the National Policy on Education. A programme for women's education and empowerment, Mahila Samakhya endeavours to create a learning environment where—

- women can collectively affirm their potential;
- gain the strength to demand information and knowledge; and
- move forward to change and take charge of their lives.

UNICEF, jointly with Public Health Engineering Department (PHED), took the initiative to build a strategic partnership with MS and facilitated promotion of sanitation and hygiene in ten districts of Bihar under the Total Sanitation Campaign (TSC) Programme involving all of their 3,598 women self-help groups for women's education and awareness.

Perseverance is the secret of excellence. If tried persistently and collectively, many things can be achieved. Mahila Samakhaya's approach, commitment and efforts have made it possible for six Gram Panchayats of Gaya district to achieve Nirmal Gram Award—Barki Chilmi in Amas block and Goitha in Banke Bazar block in 2005; Roshanganj, Saifganj in Banke Bajar block, Sawn Kala in Amas block and Angra in Dobhi block in 2006. These Panchayats are one of the most backward and poorest among poor Panchayats of Gaya district. The panchayats are located within 60 kms from the well known Buddhist pilgrim town of Bodhgaya where Lord Buddha attained enlightenment under the *'bodhi tree'*[1]. Thousands of devotees from all over the world visit this town every year. These Panchayats are also in drought prone area where agricultural production had decreased tremendously due to drought. This added to the increase in the poverty of the people. Intra as well as Inter-state migration had started in search of livelihood opportunities. Even the whole family used to migrate to other areas along with their belongings. Getting two meals a day is the main issue for the families in the Panchayats who don't foresee sanitation as an issue for them. Therefore, motivating the villagers to adopt household toilets and hygiene practices was a great challenge.

The MS follows an approach that the improvement in personal and environmental hygiene would lead to a decrease in illnesses and good sanitation would prevent major health problems for the community that too more specifically for women and children. It, therefore, intends to ensure that—

- Women, primarily, and the entire community comprehensively, understand the basic principles of hygiene and sanitation, within the home and in the community and its environs; and
- Women are empowered to participate in planning for and management of water and sanitation resources and systems to ensure their optimal and sustainable use.

Problems faced by Women due to Improper Hygiene and Sanitation Facilities in Bihar

The baseline surveys shows more than 90 per cent of women in Bihar have no options but to go out in the open for defecation. Lack of basic sanitation facilities and safe water is an acute problem for the girls and women in rural areas. Hence sanitation and hygiene are critical to the interests of women. The various difficulties faced by women due to improper sanitation and lack of hygiene practices are mainly due to the compulsion of going out in the fields before sunrise or after sunset. For this they have to curb their urges and suffer from

Box 7.1: Key Components of Women Empowerment

Women's empowerment has five components:

- Women's sense of self worth;
- The right to determine choices;
- The power to control their own lives;
- The power to handle and manage resources;
- The ability to influence the direction of social change; and create a just social and economic order nationally and internationally.

many health problems. This problem is not only related to hygiene but also to the dignity of women. Privacy is a right, which is being practically snatched away. This practice has also become a threat to their security and safety as it provides immense opportunity to many criminals to molest the honour of the women.

Many a times, grown up girls refuse to go to schools or parents do not allow them to go to school due to lack of sanitation facilities, particularly the girls from Muslim communities. During flood, the rural women wade through dirty, contaminated water and climb up a tree to relieve themselves. "I have to crawl through the mud and muck to get to the trees about a kilometre away," rued Sumitra Devi, a polio victim of Musehri block, Muzaffarpur.

MS initiatives have always been rooted in the belief in community participation, in allowing demand for development services to emerge from the community after an intensive awareness campaign. It is felt by the members of Mahila Samakhya that since women suffer most due to lack of toilets, hence, sanitation is an important women's issue. As the programme got off the ground, MS took the initiative to train women in handling the nuts and bolts of the sanitation structure. MS offers to empower rural women socially and economically through skill development by training them as masons and mechanics.

Positive Steps taken in the Implementation of TSC in Gaya

Access: The first step towards women empowerment was their access to Water and Sanitation project. UNICEF and other partners supported the principle of empowering community women in all aspects of their work. In the past community decisions were made by a small group of village leaders which almost always consisted of only men. Applying the Participatory Approach in a systematic manner opens opportunities for both women and men to be involved together in all aspects of the project. Participatory approach offered women their first occasion to discuss, plan, decide, implement and manage village action plan at par with men. Through this approach, Integrated Hygiene, Sanitation and Water Supply project has put gender equality as core objective of its community work.

Participation: The process of participation of women in Water and Sanitation projects started right from the access of women to

Water and Sanitation project. But women participation was further increased and women folk participated in a number of trainings along with men, be it training of hand pump mechanics or orientation of project managers.

Conscientisation: Women not only participated in trainings, the skills acquired during the trainings were successfully implemented in Water and Sanitation project, resulting in tremendous change in the attitude of the community.

Control: Not only women are engaged in discussing, planning or managing activities in Water and Sanitation project, they are holding important positions enabling them to take key decisions and have access to resources and manage them.

Gaya Panchayats Receive Nirmal Gram Puraskar (Award)

The six gram panchayats—Barki Chilmi and Sawn Kala (Amas Block), Goitha, Roshanganj and Saifganj (Banke Bazaar Block) and Angra (Dobhi Block) are the proud recipients of Nirmal Gram Puraskar in 2005 and 2006. While Barki Chilmi and Goitha received NGP in 2005, the rest got in 2006. Nirmal Gram Award is given to a panchayat which is 100 per cent sanitized, where all households, schools and Anganwadis have toilets and the people are well informed about the sanitation issues and practice good hygiene behaviour.

The key strategies adopted by Mahila Samakhya to achieve Nirmal Gram in Gaya were:

(a) Intensive Community Consultation and Village Planning

To mobilize the community to adopt hygiene practices and sanitation, Mahila Samakhaya started consulting the community. It was important to know their priorities and needs. The community had been consulted through Village level meetings, household visits, Gram Sabha meetings, rallies and the sanitation drives. The strategy had proved to be very effective in changing the mindset of the villagers (Fig. 7.2).

(b) Awareness Generation

Creating awareness to change personal hygiene behaviour and to keep track of the behaviour change remains, however, one of the

Fig. 7.2: Village Women from All Sections Sitting Together and Discussing Sanitation Issues

most difficult tasks. Hence in order to target behaviour changes, MS organized Hygiene campaigns targeting specific villages through awareness building activities focusing on the linkages between hygiene promotion and prevention of diseases. The messages were given to the villagers in such a way that they could understand and accept easily. 'Sanitation is a way of life' and its linkages with diseases, safety, security and health was stressed upon during awareness generation. The communities were made aware about the various technological options for sanitary toilets and the need of sanitation at household as well as the Panchayat levels. The low cost toilet models were displayed for the villagers to see and understand the technology. Village Contact Drives were organized to sensitize and mobilize the community for construction and usage of household toilets (Fig. 7.3).

(c) Village as a Unit and Mukhiya (Panchayat Head) as the Leader

MS closely worked with the panchayat members in the villages. The mukhiyas of these panchayats were motivated to lead the campaign. This approach helped MS in involving all the villagers in their efforts. Every village in a gram panchayat was perceived as a unit in itself to mobilize all the households to adopt and use toilets. All the services, such as availability of materials for construction of toilets, team of village motivators to spread the messages on hygiene and sanitation, masons to construct toilets were made available in the villages itself. The villagers did not have to travel far distances for collecting information and materials. This helped in cutting the overall cost of production and transportation of materials and the villagers could themselves get the first hand experience and knowledge of toilet construction.

(d) Empowering Women: Women as Motivator and Masons

One of the key steps taken by MS was to organize all the village women in groups. Many of the adolescent girls from these villagers were already taking part in the education programme run by MS in Gaya. At these centres, the girls were educated and empowered to take control of their own lives. They were motivated to participate and take lead in issues concerning the development of women and the village (Fig. 7.3).

In these panchayats, women were identified and trained as masons to install toilets. This also brought economic benefits to the women. The trained women masons started earning through their work. These women masons also gained social recognition. The village women found it easy and convenient to talk to women masons. These empowered and trained women masons and girls from MS centres acted as agents spreading the messages of safe hygiene habits in the community. Each member of MS led by example and constructed a toilet first in her house before carrying the message to others.

(e) Convergences of Services

To achieve Nirmal Gram it is important that not only all the families adopt household toilet and use it, but also there's separate toilet units for boys and girls in the schools and the baby friendly toilet facilities in the anganwadi centres. All the Nirmal Gram panchayats in Gaya are situated in the remotest area where development work and services have been hit hard due to threat of naxal attacks. MS efforts were instrumental in getting these services available in the villages. Apart from the availability of

Fig. 7.3: Empowered Women Masons

facilities, they also took the initiative in making the whole village environment clean. Due to their hard work, MS members have gained the confidence and support of the villagers and are respected by one and all. Their efforts have also instilled confidence among the government officials to visit these far flung places and interact with the villagers. Earlier it was a kind of distant dream for the villagers to see any government official in their village.

(f) Establish 'Mini' Production Centre in Each Village: Improved Service Delivery

Effective service delivery mechanism is vital as large scale demand for sanitation facilities are created due to intensive awareness campaign. The availability of toilet elements, such as rural toilet pans, rings, bricks, etc. was made locally so that the cost could be decreased and also to save the time. Production was also established at the village level to accelerate the construction of toilets. Local masons, especially women masons from MS, were trained to accelerate the construction of the toilets. This helped in accelerating the pace of toilet construction in the villages and more households were covered with toilets in short span of time. Due to this several women from these panchayats started earning their livelihood as trained masons working in neighbouring villages and panchayats.

(g) Monitoring Effective Use of Toilet by the Community

Since beginning MS members realized that mere construction of toilet would not bring the desired behaviour change among the families. This realization helped MS to adopt various ways to monitor that all the families in the village actually used the toilets for safe disposal of human excreta and adopted key hygiene practices of washing hands with soap, after using toilet and before handling food.

As a measure to stop open defecation, Mahila Samakhya has used an innovative mechanism. They formed an invigilation team and selected some active male and female members of the village as members of the team. The team does the invigilation duty for at least two hours adopting innovative process during early morning and evening. Their duty was to stop open defecation; if they found anyone moving towards the open field for defecation they used to stop that person by blowing whistle and sensitizing him about the ill effects of practicing open defecation and at last used to motivate that person to use household toilets. They didn't need to use force to induce behaviour change.

Lessons Learnt From Experiences on Gender, Hygiene, Sanitation and Water Supply Programmes Implemented by Mahila Samakhya in Bihar

- Gender and the role of women is a central concern in hygiene, water and sanitation.
- Specific, simple mechanisms must be created to ensure women's involvement.
- Gender analysis is integral to project identification and data collection.
- Attention to gender needs should be given as early as possible.
- Ensuring both women's and men's participation improves project performance.
- A learning-by-doing approach is more gender responsive than

a blue print approach which assumes that everything is known and can be planned in advance.

- Projects are more effective when both women's and men's preferences about "hardware/choices of technology" are addressed.
- Women and men promote project goals through both their traditional and non-traditional roles.
- NGOs and especially women's group can facilitate a gender balance approach.
- Gender-related indicators should be included when assessing project performance.
- Gender issues are important because they influence sustainability and effective use of facilities.

MS interventions have definitely paid rich dividends. The demand for sanitation facilities is growing noticeably in all the places. MS initiatives have undoubtedly shown that achieving sanitation is possible through people-centred approach based on awareness creation and women empowerment.

NOTE

1. A Banyan tree under which Lord Buddha meditated to achieve salvation.

Formation of Health Clubs

The first step in this direction was the formation of Health Clubs in all schools; the Health Clubs were envisaged as micro-level organizations responsible to conduct school health and hygiene education programmes. A Health Club consists of student representatives from each class, one teacher representative who acts as a convener and the Head Master/Principal as Chairman. Each class nominates two representatives to the school Health Club (in case of a co-education school, the representation is of one boy and one girl per class). The teacher's representative is normally the teacher who volunteers to take the lead in sanitation activities. The functions of the Health Club is to ensure the general cleanliness of the schools, toilets and washing places, placing of dustbins in classrooms and conducting sanitation related educative cultural activities. The Health Club meets once in fifteen days and reviews the performances of classes and also fixes weekly inspection schedules. It also discusses the programmes that are to be organized as part of the Total Sanitation Campaign (TSC) in schools. For monitoring and channelising two way communication between higher and lower formations the health clubs have been federated at Block level and District level. The conveners of all Health Clubs have been made members of Block level clubs and similarly conveners of Block level clubs are made member of District level committee. The district level committee is chaired by the Deputy Director (Education).

The District Sanitation Samiti under the chairmanship of District Panchayat President provided leadership to the programme at district level. The programme was implemented in the schools by the Health Clubs and PTAs. The Health Clubs were given Rs. 500-as, "one time start-up incentive" from the TSC Fund.

Training of Teachers and Conveners of Health Clubs

After formation of Health Clubs in schools, the teachers in charge of Health Clubs were provided trainings at 3 different centres. 485 teachers attended the training. The training intended at making the teachers realize that "Sanitation and Hygiene education" was not an extra curricular activity but a regular activity which required their day-to-day attention. The trainings for Health Club teachers were repeated in the following years also. On 22nd September, first period in all the schools was set apart for giving inputs on Total Sanitation Campaign to the school children who were also informed of the formation of Health Club and their responsibility in the up-keep of school cleanliness.

Training in the 1st year (1st phase) basically focused upon introduction to sanitation and hygiene education. The topics included were: salient features of Total Sanitation Campaign; duties and responsibilities of teachers; role of PTAs; organization, structure and functioning of Health Clubs etc. Training in the 2nd year (2nd phase) focused on curriculum linked sanitation education activities. During the 3rd year (3rd phase) focus was on Solid waste management and theme based IEC activities as given in Table 8.1.

Hygiene Education for Adolescent Girls

A study conducted by Dr. Anantha Kesavan, Prof. of Pediatrics Department, Thrissur Medical College among adolescent girls in 2003 revealed that the average school attendance of adolescent girls was less than that of boys. One reason attributed to the lower attendance was that the girls normally skipped school during menstruation period. The study also revealed that 50 per cent of the students suffered from headaches, stomachaches and urinary infections due to non-availability of proper sanitation facilities. In light of these findings, in order to educate adolescent girls about the importance of their personal hygiene, an educative programme was introduced for girls from 8th to 12th standard. As a part of the programme, a one day ToT (Training of Trainers) training was conducted for 250 personnel of Health and Education Department. Utilizing the services of the trained resource personnel, 48,015 adolescent girls were educated on sanitation issues of their age group.

Suchitwa Vidya—Arogya Vidya

After sensitizing the Health Clubs and school children through trainings, an effort to practice the lessons learnt was attempted in schools by promoting healthy competition among schools. A year

Table 8.1: Theme Based IEC Activities

Name of Month	*Important Day*	*Theme*	*Activities*
June	June 5 Environment Day	Monsoon and Sanitation	Water conservation, Water contamination and monsoon related epidemics. Environmental protection. Formation/Reconstruction of School Health Clubs.
July	July 11 World Population Day	Man, Earth and Sanitation	Issues related to population pressure and sanitation. Segregation of waste at source. Management and Waste utilisation.
August	August 15 Independence Day	Freedom from Waste	Freedom from waste and plastics. Poster campaign, exhibition, essay competition, suchitwa parliament. Prize distribution at Independence Day celebrations.
September	September 5 Teachers Day, September 8 World Literacy Day & Onam	Sanitation and Cultural Mode	Award to best Health Club Teachers. Cultural activities combining Onam and sanitation themes. Literacy and Sanitation.
October	October 2nd Gandhi Jayanthi	Wildlife and Sanitation	Cleanliness campaign linked to Gandhi Jayanthi – Suchitwa Padayathra's. Discussion/ Quiz competition on Zoonotic diseases.
November	November 14 Children's Day	Personal Hygiene	Emphasis on personal hygiene, Master clean/Miss clean award for cleanliness – on Children's Day.

(*Contd.*)

Name of Month	*Important Day*	*Theme*	*Activities*
December	December 25th X'mas Day	X'mas and Sanitation	Campaign against – AIDS Panparag/Drug Abuse etc. Spreading messages as part of X'mas celebrations – X'mas carols.
January & February	New Year	New Year and Sanitation. Lessons we learnt	Greeting cards design competition with sanitation messages. Hygiene related lessons at school/ class seminars/ speeches/ recitation/ skit etc

long programme was introduced during 2004 to 2005 to identify and honour the best performing schools. The following key indicators were considered by the selection committee in judging the schools:

1. Availability of drinking water
2. Availability of toilets
3. Availability of water in toilets
4. Number of separate toilets for girls and boys
5. Place for washing hands
6. Number of taps
7. Availability of water during the month of March
8. Cleanliness of toilets
9. Availability of buckets and mugs in toilets
10. Separate toilets for teachers
11. Disposal of solid and liquid waste
12. Periodicity of health inspection in schools
13. Participation of parents in sanitation programme

As part of this programme, all Wednesdays were earmarked for inspecting the nails of children. All those children whose nails were not cut used to be instructed to cut their nails then and there itself.

Awards for Best Performing Schools

As per the parameters mentioned above, 290 schools were identified as exemplary schools and were awarded mementos. Since the programme was competitive in nature, it therefore attracted whole-hearted participation of children and teachers. The mementos were sponsored by Canara Bank—the Lead District Bank. The programme had a larger objective of keeping the school community deeply involved in Total Sanitation Campaign for over a year, i.e. from 2nd October, 2004 to First October, 2005. After being involved with the programme for over a year, one notable outcome was that, the improved standards in cleanliness continued to be maintained even after the programme came to an end.

Kerala State Formation Golden Jubilee Celebration

Government of Kerala had celebrated the year 2006 as the Golden

Jubilee year for formation of Kerala state which created a festive mood throughout the state. Capitalizing upon this festive mood, Total Sanitation Campaign, Thrissur launched intensive IEC through Kalajathas. In almost 160 schools of the district, shows were staged and children gave a rousing reception to the Kalajathas. The elements of satire in the dramas stimulated their thoughts leading to correct development of habits.

Summer Camps

The Kalajathas had done their role; the once dry and uninteresting sanitation subject began to interest the school children. Camps were organized by Total Sanitation Campaign in selected schools to promote the participation of children in sanitation programmes and develop interest in socially useful periodic work. The response was tremendous; children of the camps participated in group discussions, designed posters, drew cartoons, scripted dramas and set examples. As part of Socially Useful Periodic Work (SUPW) children of the camp took part in testing the quality of water in the wells of the neighbourhoods.

Parent Teacher Association and Mother Parent Teachers Association

Any effort made in the schools shall yield the desired results only with the whole hearted co-operation of the PTA. Special meetings of the PTA representatives were conducted to apprise them of the TSC programme and for putting social pressure on the managements through PTAs to create necessary sanitation facilities. Such meetings could succeed in changing the mind set of parents who had once preferred buses, computers etc. over sanitary toilets.

Sanitation Ballot

Curiosity is the mother of invention. In India when only elders go for casting their vote in elections, children look at it very curiously. Total Sanitation Campaign, Thrissur realized the enormous potential in this curiosity of children and designed an educative programme "Vote for Sanitation". The programme enabled them to queue up, to receive a ballot paper and vote for their sanitation habits. The specimen of the sanitation ballot is as given in Table 8.2.

About 1,50,000 children participated in the voting and the findings of the poll are as per Table 8.3.

The results of the poll shows that the ballot was "thought provoking," it helped children in identifying and distinguishing good and bad habits and it facilitated switching over to the good habits.

Community Based Diseases Surveillance Programme

The reoccurrences of communicable diseases has become a regular feature and a matter of concern. In the management of these diseases, the curative mode continues to receive more attention almost neglecting the preventive part. However, when the medical science had its limitation in managing the recent viral fever (Chikkunguniya) through medicines, the focus shifted to the preventive part. It was in

Table 8.2: Suchitwa Ballot

1. The drinking water I use is	From wells	Boiled water	From pipe
2. For excretion I use	Sanitary latrine	Public place	Private open space
3. I wash my hands after excretion	Using water	Using soap and water	Using tissue paper
4. I wash my hands before and after meals	Using only water	Using soap and water	Do not wash
5. I	Grow nails	Cut nails regularly	cut nails but not regularly
6. I dispose waste	By burying	Throwing	Composting
7. I shall: Good habits	Continue	Stop	
Bad habits	Stop	Continue	

Table 8.3: Findings of the Shuchitwa Ballot

Use of boiled water	64%
Using sanitary latrine	96%
Use of soap for washing	76%
Habit of cutting nails	90%
Waste disposal by strumming	18%
Safe disposal	82%
Vector control measures	90%
Willing to stop bad habits	96%

this context, that the potential of children taking up the role of surveillance in and around their surroundings was realized and a weekly monitoring programme for 52 weeks was introduced in all the schools of Thrissur District. School children have been issued monitoring cards for recording their weekly observations which in turn are being examined by the class teachers. Based on the observations, the areas where attention of the health officials is required are intimated by the schools. As part of this programme, the health officials could be updated of vector sources in public places. The programme had a larger objective of educating children and parents of the sources of vectors and it induced them to destroy sources within their households. Specimen of the monitoring card is given in Table 8.4.

Children's Theatre

Children, who felt sanitation as a dry and uninteresting subject few years back, are now feeling otherwise. Now they have joined hands with the TSC and have come forward to participate in the IEC programmes under TSC. As part of pre-monsoon cleaning drive, as many as 10 schools conducted summer camps and scripted interesting messages on sanitation for the general public in the form of dramas and road shows. As many as 100 shows were staged during May 2008. One Drama "Speaking Garbages" created by the Children's theatre of Kerala Agriculture University (KAU), School won the national award for best drama in school competition.

Table 8.4: "Monitoring Card" "Community Based Disease Prevention Surveillance Programme"

Name of Student:		Class:			School:					
Sl. No.	Spotting Possible Mosquito Breeding Places.	1	2	3	4	5	7	up to	52	Notes
1	Is there water logging in and around your house; If Yes, did you spot larva of Mosquitoes?									Column number 1 to 52 are marked "Y" for Yes and "N" for No by the children on a weekly basis. Children were advised to destroy the sources if any, on identification and report "N". In case of public places were "Y" is recorded and authorities are informed accordingly.
2	Are there coconut shells, plastic containers, cups etc. lying in your house premises; If Yes, did you spot any larva of mosquitoes?									
3	Is there any water in the un used rubber tyres; If Yes, did you spot any larva of mosquitoes?									
4	Is there water in the terrace and sunshades of your house; If Yes, did you spot any larva of mosquitoes?									
5	Is there any water accumulation in fridges, coolers, unused grinding stones, etc., If Yes, did you spot any larva of mosquitoes?									
6	Is there water logging in the public drainage system; If Yes, did you spot any larva of mosquito									
	And other 12 more questions facilitating identification of sources.									
	Signature of Parent									Signature of Teacher

Construction of School Toilets

Apart from IEC activities, emphasis was also given in extending cent per cent toilet coverage to schools. With the support of NGOs like Centre of Science and Technology in Rural Development (COSTFORD)[1] and Socio Economic Unit Foundation (SEUF)[2] good toilet designs for schools were prepared as part of the standardization efforts. Estimate and plan for constructing toilets at a unit cost of Rs. 20,000 were prepared and handed over to the schools and Blocks for construction of toilets in schools. As many as 34 numbers of Girl Friendly Toilets have been constructed.

Trends and Expectations

Today, all the schools in the district have toilet facilities, almost all the schools have developed a flair for sanitation activities and children are forthcoming to take up socially useful work. Few examples of which are given below:

1. Water quality testing activities by students in Madakkathara Panchayat.
2. Participation of children in construction of IHHL toilets in Orumanayur Panchayat.
3. Anti-plastic campaign by KAU School students.
4. Cleaning of colonies by Perinjanam school children.

If these trends are by any way an indicator to the end results, the District expects to translate these early gains into the following outcomes:

1. Institutionalization of school sanitation programme through school health clubs.
2. Over all improvement in the cleanliness of schools and which should be sustainable.
3. Whole hearted participation of children and parents in sanitation programmes.
4. People supporting Government in its initiatives.

One major challenge was the initial reluctance on the part of the teachers and parents to teach or take part in activities which were not part of the school curriculum. However, through constant mobilization and intervention of service unions and associations such road blocks were cleared.

Unique Value

1. The programme helped the children, parents and teachers understand the full concept of sanitation and in accepting sanitation as part of their culture.
2. The programme brought in community participation.
3. It enabled schools and local bodies to work together which in turn strengthened their relationship.

Conclusion

Among IEC methods, the best method that can be adopted in schools is the cultural mode, especially street plays, skits, songs etc. as they attract the participation of children and facilitate learning through enjoyment. However, the campaign strategies having elements of both *mass education activities* like Kalajathas, dramas, paintings, lectures, demonstrations and *individual child centred education activities* like the monitoring card exercise, nail cutting exercise, *suchitwa* ballot are likely to be more sustainable. Sanitation and Hygiene education in schools has to be a continuous education programme, otherwise the gains made may regress. Finally, the programme should be planned and implemented with resoluteness, and it should not be an extemporary exercise.

Source of data: Census 2001, Deputy Director of Education, School Sanitation Base Line Survey.

NOTES

1. COSTFORD is an organization promoting research in low cost buildings and housing.
2. Socio-economic unit foundation is a voluntary organization in the field of drinking water and sanitation.

9

Better School Sanitation and Hygiene Education is an Effective Tool to Reach Community

A Case Study

V.V. Pant and *A.K. Singh*

The Convention on the Rights of the Child spells out the basic human rights that children everywhere must have: right to survival, right to development, right to protection and right to participation. Children are the future generation of the society. They have the right to grow in a clean and healthy environment. The attitude and behaviour towards cleanliness can be inculcated in the early stage of life, so school is the best platform for learning about health and hygiene related issues. Children can be the best agents to communicate the messages of good sanitation practices and environmental care in the community. Water supply and toilet facility and sanitation and health-hygiene education in the schools are the most important interventions amongst all the social sector development programmes.

Varanasi district is situated in the eastern part of Uttar Pradesh. Holy rivers Ganga and Varuna pass through the district. The Total Sanitation Campaign was launched in the district in the year 2000-01. In a densely populated district with low literacy and high poverty level, where sanitation is not seen as priority, it is always very difficult to motivate the community to construct and use toilets. Considering this as a major challenge, a strategy was formed to reach the community through schools.

Initiatives Taken in School Sanitation and Hygiene Education (SSHE)

It all started with the micro-planning for school environment, creation of child friendly sanitation facilities and initiation of their cleaning and maintenance system. Various hygiene education activities related to inculcating sanitation and hygiene behaviour among children were strategized for schools. For this purpose a base-line survey was conducted for every school in the district to get basic information on enrollment of children as well as availability, uses, and operation and maintenance (O&M) system of water and sanitation facilities in schools. In Varanasi district, out of 1115 schools only 797 have toilets along with hand-washing facilities through running pipeline water supply. The biggest achievement of SSHE was perhaps to involve children in not only imbibing the improved personal hygiene practices but also to carry the message home and share it with the parents and siblings. The members of school sanitation clubs (280 such clubs) in Primary and Junior High Schools across the district were assigned duties to keep their schools surrounding and toilets clean, which they have taken very seriously and are continuing the good work. A Knowledge, Aptitude and Practices (KAP) study on school sanitation, health and hygiene was carried out to analyze the current situation. PRI members and a teacher from every school were trained on various aspects of SSHE. A KAP status study was carried out by Divisional Water and Sanitation Coordinator (DWSC) from June 2008 to October 2008 to assess the impact of SSHE in 30 schools across the Varanasi district. The data collected dealt with the indicators like drinking water sources, washing hands before MDM[1], washing hands after using toilets, number of students having toilets at their homes, personal hygiene, monitoring of school sanitation programme, etc. (Fig. 9.1)

During the KAP study, 30 schools were covered for interviewing the teachers and students. One teacher was selected from each school. For selection of students, systematic random sampling procedure was used and all the students enrolled in the Primary and Upper Primary Schools were listed. Twenty students were selected from schools with a strength of up to 200 students. In schools having more than 200 students, 10 per cent of all the enrolled students were selected to study the behavioural changes resulting due to SSHE initiative.

Fig. 9.1: Hygiene Education among Children

Innovations

It was observed that school toilets were generally not in use. To analyze the reasons behind toilets not being used, a spider mapping exercise was carried out amongst community, students, teachers and PTA members. It was observed that apart from other minor hardware defects, lack of sufficient water for toilet cleaning was the major concern. To overcome this problem, the only remedy was to provide running water supply in the toilets. Considering this, an innovative design of converting existing India Mark II hand pump into Force and Lift Hand Pump (FLHP) was introduced. The hardware components, which included extension of water supply pipelines through FLHP in each toilet and urinal blocks along with 4-6 taps for hand washing, were provided in 797 schools in Varanasi district. In addition to toilet, urinal and hand washing facilities, the PTAs accepted and constructed soakage pits and garbage/compost pits to dispose of liquid and solid wastes (Fig. 9.2).

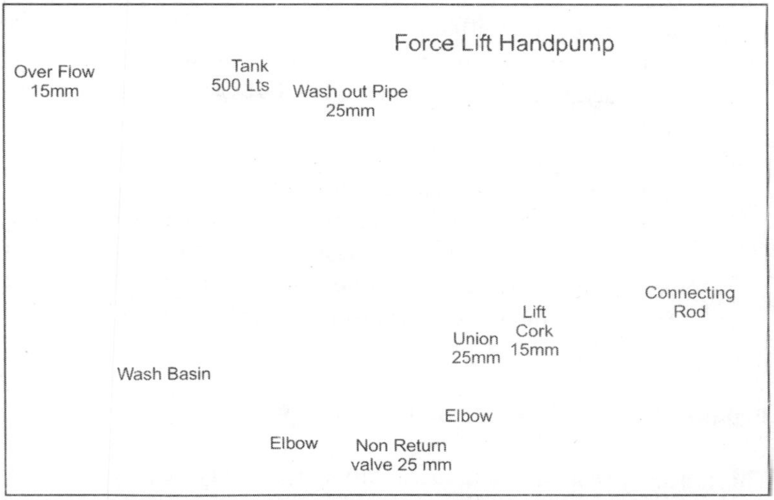

Fig. 9.2: Schematic Drawing of a Force and Lift Hand Pump

Convergence

Creating toilet and urinal facilities in the school premises alone is not sufficient to fulfil the overall objectives of SSHE. So, to inculcate safe hygiene behaviour, especially use of toilets and hand washing at critical times, amongst students it is necessary to have convergence of resources with other programmes and departments.

- *Mid Day Meal*—Mid day meal scheme can play a significant role in inculcating safe hygiene behaviour before eating. For this purpose, integration of both hardware and software activities are important. Hand washing facility with sufficient water points may be created within the school campus, and with the help of School Sanitation Club behavioural change in hand washing can be ensured.
- *Panchayat Fund*—As the fund provided for toilet unit construction under TSC is limited and sufficient only to construct toilets and urinals. But for putting ceramic tiles in urinals, FLHP, running water supply, hand washing facilities, etc. additional fund is required, and for this purpose convergence with other programmes is a must. To overcome

this problem an effective use of Panchayat fund especially 12th Finance Commission Grants provided to the Gram Panchayats was ensured at the level of Gram Panchayat and schools.

- *School Fund*—Teachers can play an important role in imparting proper hygiene education amongst students and also for regular use and proper maintenance of sanitation facilities. To overcome this issue proper coordination with education department is required. School fund may be utilized for purchasing the sanitation-related consumables (Figs. 9.3 and 9.4).

Primary School of Village Shankerpur: A Case Study

This is a story related to school sanitation in Primary School of village Shankerpur, Block Chiraigaon, situated 12 km away from its district headquarter, Varanasi. The students' strength of the school is 456. Before implementation of TSC, the school had three class rooms, two toilets and one India Mark II hand pump with no boundary wall and urinals. Apart from this, hygiene education was totally missing. Students hardly washed their hands before mid-day meal (MDM) was served and used to urinate around the toilet block. Toilets used to be choked and absenteeism amongst the girl students was high

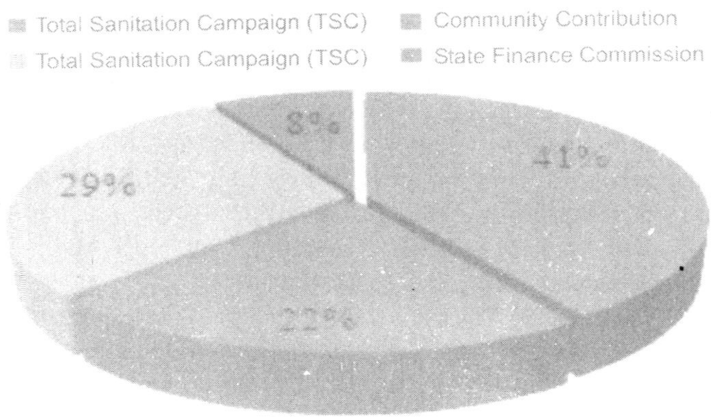

Fig. 9.3: Pie chart representing financial contribution from various sources (Total fund: 14,13,086 Indian Rupees)

Fig. 9.4: Dinning Shade Constructed by Gram Panchayat with Convergence of resources

especially after lunch. Very few students were having toilets at their homes. And teachers were also not concerned about improving sanitation and hygiene. Overall the situation was very unhealthy and unfriendly to the children (Fig. 9.5).

Then Mr. Sunnar Yadav, Gram Pradhan of Shankarpur came in the picture. He is a motivated, dedicated and committed individual. He took up the task of making the village open-defecation free, but it was very difficult for him to identify the place from where to begin this task. Mr. Yadav, Gram Pradhan of Shankarpur welcomed the idea of taking up various awareness-generation programmes involving students and help them understand some basic issues related to personal hygiene and general cleanliness in the Primary Schools of Shankarpur. He planned to begin from an old temple, which was being worshipped by the whole village community and coincidently it was located within the school campus.

He renovated the temple, but since people and children used to urinate all around it always there was a foul smell. So he asked school teachers to prevent students from urinating in the school campus. As a start up activity in school sanitation programme, school environment map was prepared by students, teachers and members of the Village

Fig. 9.5: Hand Wash before Meals

Education Committee (VEC). Existing infrastructure such as classrooms, Anganwadi centre, kitchen, water and sanitation facilities, school boundary, school garden, etc., were shown on the map. This whole process was facilitated by sanitation coordinators. Preparation of this map helped in taking up a detailed situational analysis, which paved the way for preparation of school environment micro-plan (Figs. 9.6 and 9.7).

After situational analysis, components of school environment micro-plan were implemented. It included running-water supply in toilet and urinals along with water storage facility, hand washing facility especially before mid day meal, proper maintenance of toilets and urinals, demand for extra urinal units, separate toilet and urinals for girls and boundary wall, underground drainage facility, proposal for school garden, playfield and games facilities, formation of sanitation club, community monitoring tools, etc. Apart from the wall paintings (Fig. 9.6) and slogan writings on water and sanitation issues and other activities for the joyful learning environment in the school were carried out.

Fig. 9.6: Painted wall in the school toilet

Fig. 9.7: Water storage tank connected with FLHP

All Information, Education and Communication (IEC) activities including *prabhat pheri*, celebration of monthly sanitation day, thematic competition, meeting of parents teachers association (PTA), daily monitoring of sanitation practices in the prayer class, orientation of sanitation club, etc., were included in micro planning.

Under the School Sanitation and Hygiene Education Programme of the Total Sanitation Campaign an amount of Rs. 35,000 was given to the Gram Panchayat for the construction of a toilet unit, extension of urinal and a baby-friendly toilet unit for Anganwadi centre operating from the campus. The construction work started but the fund was not sufficient enough for fixing ceramic tiles on the floors of the toilet and urinals, and for force and lift hand pump (FLHP), overhead tank, running water supply and hand washing facility. So, the Gram Panchayat decided to take up the remaining work from its own resources available under the 12th Finance Commission grants, which is a fund given to the village-level local bodies (i.e. Gram Panchayats) for operation and maintenance of water supply and sanitation facilities.

After two months of hard work, the school was provided with FLHP and group hand washing facility, separate toilet and urinal facilities for boys and girls, toilet for Anganwadi Centre with running water supply. Toilet units were beautifully decorated with child-friendly attractive wall paintings. Apart from these hardware construction activities, software activities were carried out by village motivator, which includes formation of School Sanitation Clubs, strengthening of Child Cabinet (*Bal Sansad*), monitoring of personal hygiene behaviours, sanitation drives, rallies, competitions, etc. School Sanitation Club, Shankarpur, has been formed, with each class selecting its own representative to the Club. The Club members have elected their own president. The nodal hygiene teacher advises the Club members and the PTA regularly for upkeep and maintenance of hardware facilities. The Club meets once a week (Saturday) to discuss SSHE goal. The minutes are recoded and presented to the Village Education Committee (Fig. 9.8).

Now all the school-based groups are functional and active. School Sanitation Club is sincerely involved in monitoring proper upkeep of toilet and school environment on rotation basis. Club members ensure monitoring of personal hygiene behaviour especially nail cutting and washing hands.

After these initiatives now school toilets are properly used and maintained. Students wash their hands with soap after defecation and before taking Mid Day Meal. Personal hygiene behaviours are being monitored regularly. Now the community has even installed a

Fig. 9.8: Hand Washing Facility—MDM

submersible pump in place of FLHP, on its own. Now overall school environment is clean and green.

NOTE

1. Mid-day Meal.

10

Sanitation Awareness, Assessment, Action for Schools Campaign

A Case Study from Medak District

Jai Prakash

Background

Andhra Pradesh, with a population of 762.10 lakh and area of 2,75,069 sq. km, is spread over 23 districts. The state has vast cultural and geographical diversity with three major regions—Telangana, Rayalseema, and Coastal Andhra. Medak district, situated in the semi-arid Telangana region, has an area of 9,699 sq. km and a population of 26.70 lakh. The annual rainfall in Medak is 870 mm. The ground water situation in the district is grave with 22 of the 45 mandals being declared as overexploited and critical. Water is hence a scarce resource and becomes a critical factor influencing the success of any sanitation intervention. The literacy rate in the district is only 53.24 per cent. Nearly half of the population being illiterate, the district presents a challenge in terms of the WATSAN[1] communication.

Medak has 2,648 government schools. Of these, 62.61 per cent have sanitation facilities, and among these, the percentage of schools where these facilities are usable is even lesser. In the rest of the schools, the facilities are damaged and abandoned.

UNICEF *Field Office*, Hyderabad, has been supporting School Sanitation and Hygiene Education (SSHE) under the Total Sanitation Campaign (TSC), in the district through the District Water and

Sanitation Mission (DWSM). The strategy adopted under the SSHE in the district focused largely on training of teachers to sensitize them to the importance of WATSAN and to integrate WATSAN messages into their teaching. IEC materials (teachers' manual, posters, etc.) on WATSAN were also developed and distributed to the schools in the district.

The State Water and Sanitation Mission (SWSM) has been working quite aggressively to provide WATSAN facilities in all the government schools in the state. One of the areas that the Mission focused on has been the design of child-friendly toilets. As part of this effort, the Mission commissioned a study of the status of the WATSAN facilities in three districts of the state—Medak, Anantapur and Visakhapatnam—each representing one of the three regions of the state.

The study '*Participatory Assessment of Water and Sanitation Facilities*' was designed and conducted by the Centre for Environment Education (CEE) in consultation with Sarva Shiksha Abhiyan to cover 33 schools in the state (12 of these schools were from Medak district). The study showed that the urinals in 45 per cent and toilets in 75 per cent of the schools were not in use. In 50 per cent of the schools the water supply system was dysfunctional (broken or lost taps and pipes). The availability of water was found to be the most important factor influencing the use of these facilities. The other major problems cited were faulty construction; vandalism; lack of a clear management system; and lack of awareness on the importance of WATSAN among the children, the community and the government departments. An important finding was that, in most cases only minor repairs and actions stood between the disuse and use of the existing WATSAN facilities. These repairs and/or actions usually cost very little money, but they were not being done due to a lack of initiative on the part of the school and/or the community. It was thus felt from the study that a campaign was needed to revive the existing WATSAN facilities. Rather than continuing to focus on teacher training alone, it is necessary to help the school and its community to identify and solve problems preventing full use of the existing WATSAN facilities. This realization led to the design of *SAAAF Schools Campaign* by DWSC, UNICEF and CEE. The *SAAAF Schools Campaign* stands for *Sanitation, Awareness,*

Assessment and Action for Schools Campaign. This was designed as a time-bound project to be implemented in 500 government schools of Medak district in the academic year 2006-07.

Objectives

The objectives of the *SAAAF Schools Campaign* were set forth as follows:

- To create awareness and to bring about attitudinal and behavioural changes among students, teachers, community and concerned line departments;
- Facilitate a school-level assessment of the sanitation and hygiene infrastructure use and maintenance through a participatory process involving students, teachers, headmasters, community representatives and concerned line departments; and
- Identify and initiate action at individual, school, community and line department levels to resolve problems to ensure proper use and maintenance of WATSAN facilities.

The focus on assessment and action in addition to awareness was a clear shift in strategy from the time when the 'soft-ware' interventions in SSHE were limited to awareness alone.

Salient Features

The main features of the *SAAAF Schools Campaign* are:

- School is the unit of intervention and action at the school level is desired and necessary. The focus of the project is on achieving perceptible changes in every targeted school. The status of use and maintenance of WATSAN facilities in a school covered by the project would show a clear positive change as evident in the 'Before-After' situation.
- School-specific actions are identified through an assessment process. It follows from the belief that there cannot be 'one-size-fits-all' actions for revival and use of WATSAN facilities.

The problems in each school are unique, and hence, assessment must precede action.

- There may be multiple actions requiring multiple actors. Very rarely a single action taken will spur the school into use and maintenance of its WATSAN facilities. Often many actions—some small and some significant in terms of the effort and resources required—are necessary involving students, parents, teachers, panchayats, departments, etc.
- Focus of action is on revival of existing infrastructure rather than creating new infrastructure: The project focused only on those schools where WATSAN facilities (toilets and water facility) were in existence but were in disuse. The idea is to put existing facilities to use rather than spending resources on creating new facilities that may not be used.
- Community involvement in assessment and action is necessary, as several of the issues identified pointed the need for community involvement. An often cited problem was vandalism of the school infrastructure during non-school days. On the more positive front, the schools that had excellent use and maintenance of WATSAN facilities had benefited from community support such as donations, filling up the school water tank during non-school hours, etc. Hence, it was identified that community support was both necessary (to avoid negative outcomes) and desirable (to enhance positive involvement).
- Participation of both the relevant government departments, Education and Rural Water Supply (RWS): The RWS designs and commissions school WATSAN infrastructure, while the Education department ensures proper use and maintenance of the facilities. However, lack of interaction at the ground (school) level between these departments means that the infrastructure created may not be in tune with the needs of the school (the study pointed out that in certain schools the headmasters were not consulted even on the location of the toilet). The project brings these two entities together at the school level.

Stakeholders and Roles

The *SAAAF Schools Campaign* is a multi-stakeholder initiative involving the stakeholders (see Table 10.1).

The Process

The flow-diagram (Table 10.2) shows process of *SAAAF Schools Campaign*.

Key Activities

The key activities taken up under the *SAAAF Schools Campaign* are:

I. Sensitization of Key Stakeholders from the Relevant Government Departments

While the departments of Education and RWS have been directly involved in promoting WATSAN in schools, there were several aspects on which further sensitization was necessary. The study *Participatory Assessment of Water and Sanitation Facilities* pointed the need for sensitizing the departments on:

- Attention to details in provision of child-friendly WATSAN facilities.
- Coordination amongst both departments to ensure that user needs and locale-specificity are given priority in planning for WATSAN facilities.
- Emphasis on the use and maintenance of facilities after their construction.
- Emphasis on motivation to ensure that any trouble-shooting at the school level is promptly attended to by the school and/or the community.

In order to meet the above-mentioned needs, a one-day district-level workshop was organized. The participants included the District Education Officer (DEO), selected MEOs, and selected engineers of the RWS. A detailed presentation of the key findings of the *Participatory Assessment of Water and Sanitation Facilities* along

Table 10.1: Stakeholders and their Roles in SAAAF Schools Campaign

Stakeholders (individuals, groups or institutions)	*Role of the stakeholder in the SAAAF Schools Campaign*
Students	Involvement in participatory assessment of the school WATSAN facilities and their use and Responsibility for use and maintenance of facilities by working as student committees as identified in Action Plan.
Headmaster and Teachers	Involvement in the SAAAF Campaign School Level Workshop and preparation of Action Plan; Facilitating use and maintenance of WATSAN facilities through student committees as identified in the Action Plan; Coordination with Total Sanitation Campaign, District Water Sanitation Mission, Medak, and the department of Rural Water Supply; and Monitoring.
Parents	Involvement in participatory assessment of the school WATSAN facilities and their use and Contributing to material and/or financial support for undertaking the actions identified during the assessment.
Panchayat	Involvement in participatory assessment of the school WATSAN facilities and their use and Contributing to material and/or financial support for undertaking the actions identified during the assessment.
Centre for Environment Education	Project design; Development of the module for the SAAAF Campaign School Level Workshop; Training of school-level workshop organizers; Monitoring; and Documentation.
Total Sanitation Campaign, District Water Sanitation Mission, Medak	Inputs to project design; Financial support for the project; Logistical support for project implementation; Coordination with departments of Education and Rural Water Supply; and Monitoring.
UNICEF, Hyderabad Field Office	Inputs to project design and Monitoring

(Contd.)

Stakeholders (individuals, groups or institutions)	*Role of the stakeholder in the SAAAF Schools Campaign*
Sarva Siksha Abhiyan, Department of Education, Government of Andhra Pradesh	Coordination with department staff at mandal level (Mandal Education Officers [MEOs], Mandal Literacy Officers, etc.) through the district level office; and Identification of Mandal Resource Persons (MRPs) for deployment as organizers of the SAAAF Campaign School Level Workshop.
Rural Water Supply Department, Government of Andhra Pradesh	Coordination with mandal-level staff (Block-level Engineers, etc.) through the district office.

Table 10.2: Key Processes involved in SAAAF Schools Campaign

Sensitization of key stakeholders from government departments		
↓		
School and mandal identification		
↓		
Identification of camp organizers		
↓		
Capacity building of camp organizers	↔	Development and procurement of camp materials
↓		
Organizing the SAAAF Schools Campaigns	↔	Development and dissemination of newsletters
↓		
Monitoring the progress of school-level actions	↔	Creation and management of database of actions identified through the camp
↓		
Evaluation		

with the concept of the *SAAAF Schools Campaign* was made in the workshop. Based on the feedback of the participants, it was decided that the campaign would be conducted in 20 schools in each of the 25 selected mandals of Medak covering 500 schools in all.

A second workshop was organized specifically for the MEOs of the 25 selected mandals. This two-day workshop focused on sensitizing the participants to WATSAN issues in the district and orienting them to the purpose and plan for the *SAAAF Schools Campaign*. The first day of the workshop focused on brainstorming for identifying key issues regarding school sanitation. On the second day field visits to schools were organized to examine and understand the prevailing WATSAN issues and to make school-level action plans for solving the problems. The workshop helped the participants to understand first-hand focus of the *SAAAF Schools Campaign*—identification of issues at the school level for taking action.

II. Identification of Mandals and Schools

Each MEO (from the selected 25 mandals) was asked to identify 20 schools from his/her own mandal for the *SAAAF Schools Campaign*. The criteria for the selection of schools were:

- the school should have WATSAN facility, and
- the WATSAN facility must not be presently in use.

III. Identification of Camp Organizers

District and mandal resource persons (DRPs and MRPs[2]) of Department of Education, *Preraks* of Adult Education programme and individuals from NGOs were involved. Utilizing them for the *SAAAF Schools Campaign* benefited the project in following ways:

- Being part of the education system, the MRPs were well acquainted with the school context, specifically with the strengths and limitations in the way to proper use and maintenance of WATSAN facilities.
- Nearly all MRPs and DRPs have worked as teachers in rural schools and hence are acquainted with the dynamics of school and community interactions.

Being skilled in education and training they could effectively carry out the *SAAAF Schools Campaign.*

Each MEO was asked to identify two MRPs and one DRP who could be utilized as organizers of the *SAAAF Schools Campaign*. In addition, five individuals with experience in working on WATSAN issues in non-governmental organizations were identified by the District Water Sanitation Mission, Medak. These individuals, referred to as 'facilitators' in the project, provided assistance in organizing the *SAAAF Schools Campaign* school-level workshops as well as in monitoring and follow-up. Though small in number, the facilitators were important to the project in view of their skills in mobilizing community support.

IV. Capacity Building of Skilled Individuals for Organizing the Saaaf Schools Campaign School-Level Workshops

SAAAF Schools Camp Organizers' Training

The camp organizers' training was conducted for three camp organizers from each of the 24 mandals. The participants were given hands-on experience of organizing the SAAAF workshop. To support each camp organizer at the mandal level, existing *preraks*[3] were roped into the programme. The first SAAAF workshop in each mandal was conducted by the three camp organizers from the mandal and also involved the three *preraks* of that mandal. It also served as a training opportunity for the *preraks*. The workshop focused on the three As—*Awareness*, *Assessment* and *Action*.

Awareness: Specific activities focusing on hygiene practices were conducted involving students, teachers and the community to build awareness on better sanitation practices. The activities comprised of games and group work exercises on the themes: dangers of open defecation, use of a toilet, importance of hand washing, etc.

Assessment: The assessment was done using participatory techniques involving students, teachers, headmaster, line department representatives and the community. The assessment focused on the different WATSAN facilities in school, their present status, use, reasons for non-use, the required actions to bring back the facilities into use, and the key individuals responsible for executing the action.

Action: The most important component in the SAAAF workshop is action. It involves implementing the actions identified during the assessment. Students, teachers, community, panchayat, and the line departments were the major stakeholders implementing the actions for revival of WATSAN facilities in schools. While the actions varied from school to school, the formation of student committees on WATSAN was a feature in every SAAAF school. At school level an action plan is developed using the feedback from the assessment. In all the SAAAF schools, seven different water and sanitation committees were formed. Each committee consists of about 6 students (both boys and girls) selected from senior classes. A teacher is given the responsibility of facilitating the work of each committee. Two leaders (a boy and a girl) are appointed for each committee. The committees and their roles and responsibilities are as given in Table 10.3.

On the second day of the SAAAF workshop a gramsabha is organized in the school and the prepared action plan is presented. The various stakeholders are encouraged to commit themselves to take up the required actions. The parents, the general community members and the panchayat are urged to support the execution of the action plan by providing the necessary resources. In some schools

Table 10.3: Roles and Responsibilities of the Committees

Committee	*Roles and Responsibilities*
Sanitation committee	• Encourage the students to use urinals and *WCs* • Keep urinals and toilets open during school hours • Check condition of urinals and toilets after holidays • Provide required cleaning material
Food committee	• Check the cleanliness of the utensils • Make the students wash their hands and plates • Ensure that the students follow a queue system
Drinking water committee	• Identify required repairs for the drinking water facilities • Check the quality of drinking water periodically • Ensure periodic disinfection • Provide ladles and covers • Ensure that the surroundings of the water facility are clean
Personnel hygiene committee	• Encourage and monitor personal hygiene habits in students (combing, trimming nails, washing hands with soap)
Environment committee	• Maintain cleanliness in the school • Separate wastes into degradable and non-degradable, and make compost from the degradable one • Plantation in schools and ensure after care
Class room cleanliness committee	• Maintain cleanliness in classrooms
Financial committee	This committee comprises of the Headmaster and the leaders of other committees. Its responsibilities are: • To ensure that adequate funds are collected and made available to meet the requirements of all the other 6 committees (e.g. the money required to buy soaps, broom sticks, etc.). The committee collects finances from the students, community and the visitors of the school.

funds were collected for repairs, purchase of soaps and cleaning material. Commitments are also made by the students, teachers, headmaster, line department personnel and the community for initiating and sustaining the actions planned. In most schools, the student WATSAN committees took oath during the Gram Sabha.

IEC Materials

Each camp organizer was provided with a camp organizer's manual to help in facilitating the SAAAF workshop and camp kits. The manual gives a detailed programme schedule and instructions for organizing the various components of the SAAAF workshop. The manual also contains the assessment format and the action plan format. One of the action plan formats is for display in the school and the other is to be sent to the project facilitation office for documentation. The camp kit consists of a H_2S vial for checking the bacterial contamination of drinking water, a soap to demonstrate the hand washing, charts, and sketch pens.

Monitoring

Monitoring is an important project component that has been planned and institutionalized at all the levels. At the school level, the students' WATSAN committees functioning under the guidance of teachers ensure the use and maintenance of school WATSAN facilities. The implementation of SAAAF action plan is monitored by the panchayat and the MEOs. Monitoring visits were conducted by the facilitators to the schools involved in the project. Periodic review meetings were conducted, after the school visits, with the facilitators and the line department officials, to identify and act on the issues identified.

Critical Elements that made a Difference

The first critical element that made a major difference in the process was the involvement of Education Department. For the first time the MRPs and DRPs were involved in the process directly in schools, which has influenced the process to a great extent. Utilizing them for organizing the SAAAF workshops was useful as they could give

Glimpses of Action

T. Manaiyya the Headmaster of UPS Gunthapally, Kodur mandal, feels that the SAAAF Campaign has helped to promote better hygiene practices among students. During the SAAAF camp, the drinking water in the school was tested for microbial contamination and was confirmed safe. The urinals were cleaned and made fit for use. Two pits were also dug for segregated disposal of solid waste. Student committees were formed to monitor and encourage good sanitation behaviour among students. The SAAAF camp also helped to garner community support to the school's efforts. The women's self help groups in the village donated soaps to the school for promoting hand washing.

In UPS Ankinapally, Pulkal mandal, as part of the assessment conducted during the SAAAF camp, the teachers and students identified problems related to the WATSAN facilities and the practices of students. The action plan was prepared and discussed with the village Sarpanch. As a result, the lavatory unit was cleaned and repaired, water connections to the facilities were reinstalled, and pits were dug for segregated disposal of solid waste.

In UPS Indirammanagar, RC Puram mandal, as a result of the SAAAF campaign, the Sarpanch made arrangements to repair the damaged gate and the compound wall because of which the school had problems with stray animals. Another issue identified was the height of the toilet walls. As a new double-storied building had come up near the toilet facility, the toilets were not being used by the students especially girls. After the camp the height of the toilet was raised and the facility has been brought back to use. The school premises were also cleaned and the school has planned to take up plantation.

The SAAAF Schools camp was conducted in the UPS, Thellapur. The village Sarpanch supported cleaning the school premises, the toilets, etc. The student committees were also formed and the finance committee has started raising funds to purchase soap for hand washing. Fifth class students collected one rupee each for purchasing soap and cleaning materials.

The major problem that existed in Raipahad UPS of Pulkal was with the drinking water facility. The school had no water connection. This issue was brought to the notice of the Sarpanch during the

SAAAF camp. Following this, the Sarpanch made arrangements to repair the existing facility and provided water supply to the school. A gramasabha was organized in the school and it was decided here that direct water connection would be provided in the school after the construction of the new water tank was completed. The camp organizers with the help of the community and the school students cleared all the bushes in the school premises.

Conclusion

The SAAAF Schools Campaign has brought out a new approach and new way of looking at school sanitation programme. It is clear that the schools or the concerned departments have taken school sanitation seriously. Though efforts are made time to time to improve the situation here and there, the situation remains more or less the same unless and until school and the community try to own the school including the WATSAN facilities. Involvement of all stakeholders is essential to improve the situation.

SAAAF is a programme that has potential for replication in other districts and states as well. Mainstreaming this programme as an approach to reviving use of existing WATSAN infrastructure in schools is necessary.

NOTES

1. WATSAN: Water and Sanitation.
2. The Department of Education had a cadre of teachers called the Mandal Resource Persons (MRPs) who are skilled in training.
3. Community mobilizers working on adult literacy.

11

Jharkhand-Unleashing New Wave of Sanitation

A Case Study of Innovative Approaches Adopted in East Singhbhum District

Nitin Kurkarni

Jharkhand, a land of forest and natural resources, has its own interesting sanitation story marked by slow but steady progress. With 23 per cent[1] coverage, it certainly lags behind in comparison to the States like Kerala or Sikkim or its neighbour West Bengal, but the way the state has engaged with sanitation drive in the last few years in scripting some of the path-breaking initiatives; has led to believe that total sanitation is possible in the State. The efforts in East Singhbhum District particularly have strengthened such initiatives. Some of cases of these initiatives of this district are shared that offers insightful learnings especially in areas like partnership with women groups in demand generation and supply chain, social mobilization, school sanitation and monitoring.

Partnership between ICDS and TSC—Chakulia Story

TSC has been actively promoting partnerships with ongoing government schemes but the way the partnership with Central Government's Integrated Child Development Scheme (ICDS) has been developed and strengthened in Jharkhand is an example. The context of Chakulia, one of the blocks of East Singhbhum district, reinforces the spirit of partnership which once upon a time was struggling on sanitation *radar* especially in demand generation activities in the absence of any credible NGOs. But the decision to involve ICDS workers in the TSC programme implementation changed everything. An average working day for an *Anganwadi sevika* or *sahayika* in the district means hours of travelling on foot, through the villages under her charge, visiting as many homes as possible and basically catering to their nutritional needs. In other words, ICDS presented a ready network of workers, those hardy, plucky women, who are no strangers to hard work, and who are in tune with needs and problems of the villagers they talk, laugh and joke with them everyday. The ICDS workers are already equipped with all the prerequisite skills in dealing with thc rural mindset, often hailing from in and around the very same villages in which they work. Having become a familiar face over the years, they have successfully managed to *allay* the natural suspicion of villagers for all things that are 'urban' or are new. Having also won the confidence of the family members, especially those who have the decision-making powers, these ICDS workers found fairly easy as they did not have to spend time in first winning the confidence and trust of these tribal families who can be extremely distrustful of strangers. The ICDS workers also scored over NGOs in that they were already familiar with the needs and the problems of the villagers and had better convincing powers by virtue of long years of association.

It all started with intensive training of sevikas across its 122 Anganwari Centres and 244 women members of the various Kishori Mandals and the Mahila Mandals with help of Devnet, Patna-based organization supported by UNICEF. The training covered the areas of masonry work, management of production centre and demand generation activities. One of the primary aims of teaching the women all the nitty-gritties was to make sure that the tempo of the TSC did not lose its speed after the government and other implementing partners withdrew after completion of the project period. The main aim was to make the project self-sustainable by training the chief players, that is, the women, who would ultimately shoulder the responsibility of the project and help carry it forward. During the intensive training period itself, these fieldworkers generated demand for 2528 BPL toilets and 121 APL toilets with the community contribution (Fig. 11.1).

Fig. 11.1: ICDS Workers Involvement in TSC Implementation

Fresh from their week-long training at the Gadra Production Centre, these women were raring to go. We were taught the basics of ring making, installation etc. and we are confident that we can do this work," said Sonali Maity, president of the Sarojini Mahila Mandal. Her sentiments were echoed by her companions, Laxmi Maity (Treasurer), Sudishtha Maity, Shikha Maity, Sandhya Das, and Abha Das. A similar response was found among the members of the Indira Mahila Mandal, ledby president Annamati Mandal, Sita Sikdar, Mousumi Singh, Badli Sardar, Jyotsna Sardar and lla Sardar.

But they had their share of problems too. According to an Anganwadi worker Ranjana Mahato, "People said that they wanted to install low cost toilets but came forward with other problems like not having received their 'red cards' and IRDP[2] and cited those as reasons for not having enough money to construct it."

After the National Review Mission held in Jamshedpur, the district administration did some serious assessment of the output produced by all the implementing NGOs and in many instances the latter cut a sorry figure in terms of not meeting targets of demand generation and subsequent installation. In fact, disillusioned with the tall claims and poor performance of many NGOs, the government is now seriously considering using ICDS as its implementing agency in all the panchayats where TSC implementation is poor. The tremendous success achieved in Chakulia can be a torch-bearer for not just other districts but for other states where TSC is in operation. The success met by ICDS in Chukulia later replicated in four other Blocks of the district and one of the Blocks has been proposed for Nirmal Block for prestigious Nirmal Gram Block (NGP) for the year 2007-08.

Also, the partnership with SHGs has played a major role in strengthening women participation in the better implementation of TSC resulting in many women SHGs taking up the production of sanitary materials as their economic activities. For example, the Mahila groups of Kasaphalia and Arand villages of Baharagora Block of East Singhbhum where for the first time *an all-women production centre* for low cost toilets has come up. Male eyes curiously follow every movement of these 12 women of the SHGs, as they load and mix sand and cement, *deftly* slap into shape the circular ring frame and then immerse the dried ones into a nearby hollow filled with water from the hand pump. These are the women of the Tara Mahila Mandal, six of who underwent five-day residential training at the production centre in Gadra, on the outskirts of Jamshedpur. The Anganwadi sevika Stella Hansda has been a constant companion to these women, encouraging them, supervising the work while simultaneously keeping the children of these toiling women busy in academic activities. Parvati Kesu, the president of this SHG for her members, "We have received fu!l support from our husbands and the other menfolk in the family. There is no domestic tension because we are doing this work."

The first batch of rings and frames started on September 23, 2003. In just three days, 21 sets were already made. Before these women took up the challenge of running their own production centre, the only source of livelihood was to buy *dhan (rice)* from the Kedulocha *haat*, have it threshed into rice and carry it all the way to Parsudih in Jamshedpur for sale. Every week, the 50-60 kilos of rice would fetch the women a meagre profit of Rs. 25-30. But now already Rs. 81,759 has been deposited as a part of the money received for the construction of toilets and this is just a beginning for them (Fig. 11.2).

Changing Behaviour and Action: Village Watsan Planning-cum-Sanitation Drive

Various planning exercises have been tested on different issues in various programmes in India but the success of village planning in East Singhbhum, a people driven approach to bring about a significant change in the quality of life through people's participation, has given all new perspective to mobilize community for the demand generation. This tool was first tried out in 2004 when TSC and Swajaldhara were scaled up district wide after release of funds from Government of India and and State Government in mid 2004. Cluster

Fig. 11.2: Rings made by SHG's

of villages were taken up for social mobilization and creating awareness through village-based motivators (mostly women), panchayat and cluster level functionaries. These community mobilizers were trained on Watsan issues and they carried out inter-personal communication. The community mobilizers are paid incentive based on 5 output indicators. The strategy paid off in creating awareness and demand for home sanitation initially. A 4-Day package of intervention was field tested with UNICEF support. The package focused on behaviour change communication and mobilizing communities for WATSAN planning.

The field trial was carried out in selected villages. The 4-Days WATSAN Planning was first field tested in Belajuri, Ghatsila in the month of April 2006 with improved demand-supply chain. The response of the drive was tremendous in terms of toilets demand and communities' willingness towards water source repairing and maintenance. Belajuri village is situated 23 km away from Jamshedpur. The *Karmakars* and *Yadavas* are the main residents of the village and their main source of income is agriculture. Before the exercise water and sanitation situation of the village was very poor. The outcome after 4-Days exercise were 40 per cent increase in demand for toilets with all 14 handpumps functional and 5 user groups formed for O&M along with the formation of Bal Sansad in all the schools.

The success of this initiative has motivated the State Government to issue administrative and financial guidelines for scaling up of WATSAN planning dovetailing resources from TSC and Swajaldhara. After experiencing the success of the field test and keeping in view the State directives, WATSAN planning was scaled up in 73 villages of East Singhbhum in 2006. The result of the 73 villages WATSAN planning provided a new IEC medium to the district and it is further scaled up in all 148 villages of targeted NGP Block of the district.

It reinforced the fact that people want to participate and there is need to develop strong communication with them. It also supported that integrated dissemination of messages on behaviour change help adoption as well as instant demand for sanitation facilities and when these are backed up with supplies result in adoption of behaviour. The orientation of school teachers and children on WATSAN can also help in generating demand from the communities.

The key of the success lied upon the clarity in the objectives which were:

- To mobilize communities on safe water and hygienic practices of sanitation.
- To empower the communities to share the responsibility for maintaining the existing water source and come forward for water supply schemes.
- To promote hygiene practices through schools with active participation of school teachers, children and community. *(SSHE)*.

The key strategies were—

- Behaviour Change Communication in families/Institutions (School/AWC/PHC/SHGs)
- Inter sector coordination (DWSD/NGO/PC)
- Community participation
- Participation of vulnerable groups
- Promoting Sanitation through school
- Participatory planning

Implementation of Village Planning

Supported by a four-member team, the central methodology—community dialogue with various tools and techniques has been used to draw community's attention towards the issues related to hygiene, sanitation and water supply. The four-days village planning exercise contains IEC activities, the tool for mass mobilization. Activities at various institutions (Village communities, School, Anganwadi, Additional Primary Health Centre (APHC) and SHGs are conducted to achieve the objectives of the exercise. In the beginning, an assessment on water and sanitation is done sitting with the villagers. The whole process is continuously backed up with communication activities. After second day people collectively become aware of their situation. The process ends up with villages' own plan to handle water, hygiene and sanitation issues. The day-wise activities versus expected outcome of the Village Planning are mentioned below:

Day-One

- *Village/communities*: Transact walk and meeting with villagers—assess WATSAN status
- Children's rally
- IEC material exhibition
- Video show and village meeting—need of toilet and its various low-cost options
- *School*: Discussion with teacher
- Orientation of Village Education Committee
- Interaction with Children and orientation for the household survey

Outcome—Orientation of villagers, school teachers and children on water and sanitation and demand for toilets.

Day-Two

- *Village/communities*: Discussion with villagers on seasonality of water and sanitation related diseases
- Village Map to understand the water source/sanitation facilities of village, Sticking posture and video shows in different locations School.
- Orientation of children on seven components with Laxman Rekha.
- Other tools *AWC:* Orientation on seven components with Laxman Rekha[3] *Community participation:* Repairing of the non-functional Handpumps by DWSD mechanics with community participation and Demand collection from the community
- *Outcome*—Demand for toilets, mobilization of villagers and AWWs on safe water and hygienic practices of sanitation and all the Handpumps in the village get functional.

Day-Three

- *Village/communities*: Orientation of the communities on the need of hygienic practices Demand of toilets, Formation of user group

- *School*: Cleanliness drive and orientation on safe water and hygienic practices of sanitation with different games and discussion with Child Cabinet on need of hygiene and sanitation

Outcome: Active Bal Sansad, formation of user group, construction of soakage pit and demand for toilets.

Day-Four

- *Village/communities*: Wall writing, drawing competition for members of Child Cabinet, orientation on community linkage, Household visit for motivation for adopting sanitation and hygienic behaviour. Village meeting—discussion on water and sanitation, formation of user group, orientation of the communities on Swajaldhara, prize distribution and preparation of monitoring board.
- *PHC*: Orientation of ANM, women group-discussion on safe water and hygienic practices of sanitation, community participation: cleaning of handpump vicinity, demand for toilets, digging of pits and construction of toilets.

Outcome—Villagers are ready for toilet installation, formation of user groups and community coming forward for Swajaldhara, developed village plan of action to solve the water and sanitation issues.

School Sanitation and Hygiene Education—Role of Child Cabinet

Bankati School is one the schools situated in Ghatsila Block of the District East Singhbhum. Only few years back, children of this school were not much concerned in attending their school, but now the whole scenario has changed and now every morning children eagerly wait for the school to open. The fascination behind this is improved school environment with all the basic facilities where children can enjoy the learning process. There are provision of drinking water, exclusive toilet for girls, gardening facilities, force lift pump, other child friendly elements—see-saw, swing, marry-go-round, child exercise and playing related equipments etc. The District administration, Jharkhand

Education Project and UNICEF efforts have shaped the school setting become child friendly to reduce drop out of children.

But the role of the child cabinet was paramount. Children's cabinets consisting of leaders heading various areas of work has been set up in the school. The common areas of work for these children cabinets are gardening, health, hygiene, sanitation, prayer, education, sports and culture, finance, etc. Care has been taken in not discriminating but dividing the responsibilities evenly between girls and boys in order to provide them with equal chance of leadership. The cabinet members meet regularly to review the progress of their work. Besides this, the teachers also participate in as much as they meet with all the members of the committee periodically to assess their work, share their observation and guide them in their forthcoming assignments. The students share their problems at this platform.

The school schedule begins with a cleanliness drive. The child cabinet minister incharge of the cleaning with the help of other children cleans toilet units, classrooms and school premises before start of the classes. The regular checking of nails during prayer by the child cabinet also inculcates hygiene behaviour among children. The cleanliness reflects far and wide in the school right from the school premises, toilet to their uniform and overall children's personality. Cleanliness and hygiene is also linked with water availability. The activity to store water in overhead tank in the toilets is also fun for the children. Before starting prayer and midday meal the students exercise with force and lift pump to store water. The children made provision for handwashing right at the corner of the handpump platform and keep soap water to clean their hands before meal. In the toilet same arrangement has been made by the child cabinet for washing hands after defecation. The cabinet contributes a tiny amount managed by *Finance Minister* for soap, broom, long handle ladle and other items for WATSAN management and hygiene promotion. In the lunch break, all the children run towards the handpump and wash their hands with soap before midday meal is provided by the school. After lunch they wash their hands again and have water using long handle ladle. At the end of the day they conclude the classes with the cleaning of their classes.

The hygiene practices developed among the children slowly linked child to child, child to parent and parent to community. Bankati village is one of the villages of Nirmal Gram awarded Panchayat

Kankrisole, where all the households have adopted good sanitary and hygiene behaviour. Bankati School has become role model for the other schools of the district. The vibrance of the child cabinet is playing important role to manage WATSAN facilities and other hygiene behaviour in their school.

Redefining Monitoring through Integrated MIS

Information system plays a crucial role in the management of any enterprise including the social sector. The fast changing scene of liberalization, competition and globalization combined with emphasis on quality, timeliness, innovation and efficiency puts a premium on accurate and timely information with adequate analysis. Computing and communication technology have indeed made such demands transferable into realizing goals.

As a part of UNICEF-GoJ collaboration, Management Information System (MIS) was conceptualized to provide quality analysis of the programme implementation, which would later be scaled up in the entire state. East Singhbhum was taken by State Water and Sanitation Mission (SWSM) as pilot district to implement MIS for all the programmes in an integrated manner. It was considered that there was a need to shift the focus from village level monitoring to household level behaviour change monitoring in terms of water and sanitation. The ongoing UP experience was also taken into account while developing the monitoring system. The concept was transcribed into a fully computerized MIS system in April 2005. The first three months were dry run phase. Since August 2005, the refined MIS has been operational in the East Singhbhum district on pilot basis and the data is being entered as the programme is expanding. The success of the MIS in East Singhbhum widened its scope and on this date the MIS has been scaled up to all 22 districts of the State of Jharkhand.

The MIS is categorized as per the national programme in three sections with the additional facilities (Import/Export and documentation templates) to make it effective and user friendly.

1. Total Sanitation Campaign (TSC)
2. School Sanitation and Hygiene Education (SSHE)
3. Swajaldhara (SD)

The key objectives were:

- To develop a tool for planning, managing and monitoring for TSC/SSHE and Swajaldhara.
- To create an effective and practical system of assessing, analyzing and generating information for action at various levels for improved water and sanitation.
- To track each and every household's water, hygiene and sanitation behaviour.
- To assess the programme status and plan future course of action.

The key features of the MIS system developed are:

- Captures changes upto the household level for both hardware and software indicators.
- Simple and user friendly.
- Handles all-important indicators for TSC/School Sanitation, and Swajaldhara.
- Built-in feature for export and consolidation of data from lower levels to higher levels.
- Provide facility for importing reports and graphics into other packages such as Word, Excel and PowerPoint presentations.
- Produce routine documents and letters, required for the execution of various programmes.
- Facilitates learning with requisite flexibility to share various types of documents, BCC and training materials.
- Dynamic query facility for analysis on various indicators; listing non-performing/performing villages/schools and so on.
- Provides a powerful reporting facility to analyze data in easy to understand tables and graphics (maps, charts etc.) The reporting is on the lines of GOI supported formats and monitoring system of TSC/SSHE and Swajaldhara.
- Report contains maps up to village level with status related to various indicators shown, helps in comparing performance.

The key indicators for the three programmes are as given below:

Total Sanitation Campaign (TSC)

- Toilet demand, construction and its use.
- Specific place for hand washing and availability of soap and water at the place.
- Hand washing practices at critical times (Before meal and after defecation).
- Use of long handle ladle or high neck pitcher to take out drinking water.
- Safe disposal of waste water (soakage pit/kitchen garden).
- Family contributing for O&M of water systems and expenditure on O&M of water systems with community contribution.
- Type of water source being used by the family.

(Also covers monitoring of production centre, Anganwadi sanitation, Community complex, rural sanitary mart/Handpump spare mart etc.)

School Sanitation (SSHE with SWASTHH Indicators)

- Use of safe drinking water.
- Separate toilet available and being used by girls.
- Availability of hand washing facility along with soap/ash are in use.
- PTA/VEC regularly meeting and proper upkeep of records (SWASTHH Indicator).
- Children forum/child cabinet engaged in hygiene promotion activities in families (SWASTHH Indicator).
- Monitoring board on hygiene regularly updated by teacher/ children (SWASTHH Indicator).
- Curriculum device linked to hygiene education available in school and being used by school teachers (SWASTHH Indicator).
- Adopted quality intervention elements (SWASTHH Indicator).

Swajaldhara

- VWSC/HWSC constituted.
- Villages/habitations planned new water supply schemes.
- Villages sanctioned with new schemes.
- Villages where water supply scheme is under construction.
- Villages where water supply scheme construction completed.
- Villages managing O&M of new as well as old water supply system.

The MIS has data collection formats for each programme which are discussed below:

Total Sanitation Campaign (TSC)

- *Family Register Format (Parivarik Swachhata Panji or Green Register)*—The baseline status of the programme for all components of TSC.
- *Community based hand pump maintenance Format (User Group or Pink Register)*—The format is to collect the information of existing/new user groups formed for the maintenance of handpumps.
- *Monthly Register Format (Masik Parivarik Swachhata Panji or Yellow Register)*—The monthly information on household sanitation behaviour and user group is collected through yellow register.
- *Nirmal Gram Puraskar Format*—The progress of the proposed Nirmal Gram Panchayat is collected in this format on household hygiene and sanitation behaviour, user group, School and Anganwadi Sanitation.
- *Production Centre Format*—The details of the production centre is collected through this format.
- *Institutional Toilets Formats*—Any new information of community toilets and existing/new Anganwadi toilet information are collected through these formats.
- *Other formats*—TSC Physical and Financial, Capacity building and mobilization and village-wise project input details are the other formats available for the data inputs.

Capacity building and mobilization format is categorized in five formats at different levels.

School Sanitation (SSHE with SWASTHH Indicators)

- *Basic and baseline Information Format*—The basic information about the school collected through this format with baseline information.
- *Monthly Information Format*—The monthly update of the school sanitation comes through this format on eight star components.
- *Other Formats*—Project inputs details and Capacity building and mobilization are the other formats available at district to collect information on school-wise inputs and meeting/ workshop and other activities details.

Swajaldhara

(See Fig. 11.3)

- *Basic Information Format*—The format is to collect data for any new Swajaldhara scheme.
- *Monthly Information Format*—The progress and the status of the scheme with components details and expenditure collected through this format.

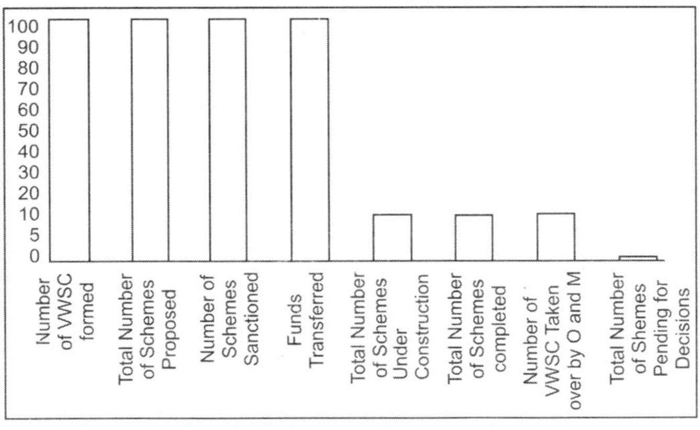

Fig. 11.3: State Graphical Report (Swajaldhara)

- *Other Formats*—Project inputs details and capacity building and mobilization are the other formats available at district to collect information on village wise inputs and meeting/ workshop and other activities details.

The MIS is used for

- Spot verification of progress reported.
- Analyzing the present status of the Programme (TSC/SSHE/ Swajaldhara).
- Evaluation of the programme pace.
- Intervention in weak areas and replicate the success of other areas.
- Details of the water and sanitation scenario up to village level.
- Fast and accurate retrieval of Reports.
- Presentation on the key output.
- Maintaining quality of the programme.
- Check on duplication of reporting.
- Information of all the stake holders with details:
  - Templates to manage the important letters, orders, guidelines and other documents related to programmes.
  - Facilitate decentralized data compilation.

Sample MIS

Currently, after the success, the MIS has now been scaled up in all the 22 districts after the 4-Days training to all the District Coordinators and Data Entry Operators. Due to this MIS, the actual number of families to be covered and families left out is always and easily available for all the agencies involved in the programme. So there is also no chance of any duplication of beneficiaries at any level as such instance is easily detected. In addition, data manipulation at any level is not possible. It has been planned to record and update of all 22 districts household water, hygiene and sanitation beheviour as well as decentralizes data compilation up to Block level and linked to information systems for development sectors. It also plans to develop progress card for the field functionaries and linkage with their payments and eventually linking the State MIS with the GOI website (www.ddws.nic.in) for automatic updating of report. All the districts in the state are using this MIS currently, but the linking with the NIC website has not been done.

NOTES

1. TSC MIS accessed on 19th September, 2009. The rural coverage was just 6.2% at the time of Census, 2001.
2. BPL families are issued PIN numbers under the then IRDP scheme. This is referred to as IRDP by the villagers.
3. Laxman Rekha is an IEC material used to sensitize participants on the 7 components of Sanitation.

12

Sanitation—A Way of Life

A Case Study from District Moradabad

Amit Kumar Ghosh

Sanitation is fundamental to all development. Lack of sanitation is a public health disaster. It consigns nearly 3 billion people across the globe—nearly two-third of them are women and children whose needs for sanitation are critical and acute—to life in primeval conditions, without access to latrines. Enhanced sanitation services represent a fundamental step towards improved living standards for poor people with special focus on women. Moreover, access to sanitation is a fundamental human right, which safeguards health and human dignity. Lack of sanitation is a social and health problem, and women suffer an additional handicap, which does not apply to men, of attending to natures call. Women in rural India, as in most parts of the world, often suffer from lack of privacy, sexual harassment and need to walk large distances to find a suitable place for defecation in the absence of household/community toilet facilities.

Going with the programme, when we started it in Moradabad district in 2003-04, was tougher as the district is situated in western UP where people are more resistant to any change and the area is thronged by a big Muslim population where percentage of illiteracy is rather more. But contrarily, it was easier to implement the programme, as the economic prosperity of the area was able to bear the cost of this new initiative.

Before going to the field for actual work, a base-line survey was conducted which included all kinds of households, those which had "proper toilet" or a dry latrine or those whose members go to the open fields for defecation. The behaviour of the individual and of the community as a whole was also studied. The mindset of the community and its response towards health and hygiene issues, including their prevailing practices, were all examined and scrutinized. The main facts that came out of the detailed survey may briefly be narrated as follows:

1. A big chunk of rural population, almost 80 per cent, was found used to the habit of open defecation.
2. About 80 per cent of Muslim households were having dry latrines, as prevalence of "Purdah System" in the community makes open defecation unthinkable for women. Men were also found using dry latrines but did not refrain from open defecation like others.
3. The condition of school toilets was poor. In most of the cases teachers used them and children were not allowed to enter.
4. The hygiene conditions were below average and a lot had to be done through information, education and communication (IEC).
5. Only those families kept their pour-flush-water toilets well kept who got them constructed by their own sources. The toilets constructed with "Indira Awas" and under other schemes launched before Total Sanitation Campaign (TSC) were, in more than 60 per cent cases, not in use. Even those who had spent money as 'beneficiary-share' had little care of their assets, as it was convenient to convert them into bathrooms just by sealing the pan.
6. The level of general cleanliness, regular health check-ups and many other things was abysmal.

Planning and Efforts

TSC's aim is not just that every household gets a toilet but its scope and goals are much larger. So, we prepared our project keeping all the fragments of the programme in our mind. Following the guidelines of TSC, we decided to provide subsidy to every BPL family that has not earlier been taken up under any other programme. We also took school toilets and IEC activities in our programme. But in the beginning, our programme was not sufficient as per the needs of the district. So in the year 2007 we revised it as per the Government of India's instructions.

Strategies and Key Resource Persons (KRPs)

1. The district decided to hand over the programme fully to Gram Panchayats and different representatives at different levels.
2. In each Gram Panchayat an ambitious, efficient and active person was selected to be the motivator.
3. At Block level, "Block Motivator" was also appointed.
4. All key departments including education, health and social welfare and Integrated Child Development Services Scheme (ICDS) were linked with the campaign.

Information, Education and Communication

The IEC strategy under TSC is very organized and linked with output. It has focused on both mass and individual campaigns. Motivators have been appointed in all the villages and it has been found that women are the main influencers. There are many themes related to women's dignity, comfort, status, operation and maintenance (O&M), cost-effectiveness, technological options, etc., which are being used. Through wall paintings, hoardings, meetings, magic shows and open discussions at different levels, an atmosphere was created throughout the rural area of the district. We took the message down to the lowest level through Pradhans, members of the Gram Panchayats, motivators, teachers, ICDS workers and any other person who could do it voluntarily.

In preliminary stage, we didn't focus on construction of a toilet in a house. Through IEC we tried to spread the message of health and hygiene to the maximum possible extent. ICDS workers formed groups of women who were rather more motivated to get the things done. Door-to-door contacts and routine meetings at Block and Village levels gave a boost to the campaign. Regular health check-ups, competitions in schools and many other things changed the mindset of the people.

Our main targets and related activities may be summarized as follows:

- Preparation of a good network of government officers, especially in Panchayati-Raj and other development departments, at district, block and village levels, and giving them definite goals and responsibilities. They were reoriented in a proper manner before they started their work.
- Preparation of an effective network of the representatives of Panchayats and other social workers at different levels. They were also given training at regular intervals.
- Monitoring system was also developed at every level.
- In the beginning, everybody discussed the issues related to health, hygiene and women dignity at every level.
- We focused on both mass and individua! campaigns.
- Motivators were appointed almost in all village Panchayats and during the first phase of campaign, it was found that the women were the main influencers. The reason is crystal clear because a personal toilet is related with women's dignity, comfort and status. Since the domestic budget remains in women's hands, they, if motivated, can easily save money to get a toilet constructed by curtailing many other expenses of less importance.
- Our most important targets were schools, especially 'Junior High Schools' with co-education. Girls of class VI to VIII are mature enough to understand the sensitivity of the programme. They got themselves organized into groups and went door to door and motivated the people for opting toilets and drinking water.

Manual Scavenging

Manual scavenging involves removing human excreta using brooms, small tin plates and baskets that are carried on the head. 'Dry latrines' are much more dangerous for families' health and invite diseases. We told the families that human excreta that remains in the house for

> Fifty-seven year old Nirmala was reborn two years ago. Condemned to a life of drudgery and indignity for nearly half a century, this manual scavenger had been carrying human excreta from the young age of eight. She bid good-bye to that miserable stage of her life only two years ago. Today she is happy and wishes to forget her 'filthy past'.
>
> Hailing from Balmiki caste, untouchables like Nirmala have for centuries been ostracized by even the other 'low-caste' Dalits and Scheduled Castes. No wonder that she had reconciled to her fate by then when a revolution overtook her village, Mohamad Ibrahimpur of Baniakhera block in Moradabad district. Under the scheme all the 600 odd village dwellings, including that of Nirmala, acquired a flush toilet.
>
> Overnight Nirmala also turned jobless. But two years down the line, the initial anxiety is over. She has now become a labourer, the only alternative left before illiterate Nirmala. Her life has started on a new note all together. She is happy and free from what Mahatma Gandhi termed as the 'hateful, inhuman, unhealthy practice' of manual scavenging.

24 to 48 hours is the root cause of diseases. Moreover, we also told them plainly that manual scavenging is a crime and ultimately we succeeded in abolishing manual scavenging to a great extent. One after another, thousands of dry latrines were converted into pour-flush-water seal latrines. We gave subsidy to those who were poor and others invested their own money. The scenario was thus changed to a great extent.

The effects of the removal of 'dry latrines' in comparatively big village Panchayats made the programme popular and helped in taking it ahead. Those who didn't have even dry latrines and were used to 'open defecation' witnessed the results. They also understood that constructing a proper toilet for them was not a costly affair. They saw affordable models and opted for them easily. We tried to make the 'pour-flush-water seal latrine' a symbol of family's dignity, and as a result many more came forward to embrace it.

Initiatives Taken for School Toilets and Aanganwadi

Under TSC, each Primary, Junior, and Higher Secondary School in rural area must have separate toilets and urinals for boys and girls. Hand washing facilities should also be there. This was the component that the district took up with most seriousness. Though Gram Panchayats and Shiksha Samities got the school toilets constructed yet we did not leave these bodies helpless. UNICEF supported Sanitation Coordinators, and Deputy Director (Panchayati Raj) and other officials devised various innovative and attractive models of school toilets and got them constructed with great zeal. Every toilet was given 'water facility' with the help of force-lift hand pumps and water tanks.

Similarly, model Aanganwadi toilets were constructed. It was clarified that they must be used by the children and teachers both. Some school toilets were of the kind that people from surrounding areas still come to see them. This gave a good message and people began to think of giving up the habit of open defecation. Children especially girls, who used toilets at school, insisted their families to have the 'same ones' in their homes. This strategy helped the campaign to a large extent.

Nirmal Gram Puraskar (NGP)

Uttar Pradesh is one of the 14 states in India to receive Nirmal Gram Puraskar in 2005. The NGP was launched by the Government of India in 2004. NGP is given to the Panchayats which are 100 per cent sanitized, where all the households have toilets, each school and Aanganwadi has toilets and the people are well informed on hygiene habits and practice them well. Moradabad district received its first NGP in 2004 for two of its Gram Panchayats. In 2005, the number went to 25 Gram Panchayats.

People with a Difference...

Little Shabana's eyes sparkle with joy every time she talks of the new flush latrine constructed just last month inside her little hutment. She will now no longer have to undertake those arduous journeys at unearthly hours to answer nature's call.

Tammana's village Akka Delari, in Munda Pandey block of Moradabad district in the state of Uttar Pradesh, is one of the 40 villages from Uttar Pradesh in the year 2005 to receive NGP presented annually by the President of India for total rural sanitation, which includes zero open defecation.

Lessons Learnt

Through our campaign we have learned some valuable lessons in the process:

- Investment in children, as change agents and health ambassadors, has shown remarkable results in persuading the family and community to build toilets and adopt appropriate sanitation behaviour.
- The absence, inadequacy of toilets in schools, particularly for girl children is a major challenge to educating the girl child and in using the school as a catalyst for hygiene and sanitation.
- The role of women is a central concern in hygiene, water and sanitation.
- Ensuring both women's and men's participation improves the campaign.
- Attractive slogans, wall painting, message-giving pictures attract the people a lot and help in changing the mind set.

We still have to do a lot. It is not a construction work but a campaign. It is a movement against century-long tradition of open defecation of man-kind. The increasing literacy may also be helpful in ending open defecation, but we must remain alert that what has been done must sustain and go forward. New generation has to be focused more and more so that our future problems get lessened. In the end, I would like to say that sincere efforts may delay the results but will never have to face failure.

13

Total Sanitation Campaign and Its Impact on Rural Health

A Case Study from East and South Sikkim

Vishal Mukhia

Introduction

Sikkim being a mountainous small state of the Indian Union, large tracts remained isolated for quiet a long time due to difficult terrain and topography. It encompasses a total area of 7,096 sq.km with its geographical profile ranging from low lying deciduous plains to snow covered alpine mountains. Majority of the population live in rural areas in the state and the total population as per 2001 census is 5,40,493. When Sikkim became the twenty second state of India, the State had very limited development space both in economic and political sense. The onset of Democratic Decentralization and building of economic structures changed the entire profile of Sikkim. From a traditional economy with feudal slant, Sikkim has emerged as a modern and robust state.

The Total Sanitation Campaign views the sanitation problem holistically and looks at important tools and approaches that create demand for sanitation. It was in this context, with the support of the Department of Drinking Water Supply, Ministry of Rural Development, Government of India, Government of Sikkim launched Total Sanitation Campaign (TSC) Programme in Sikkim from the financial year 1999-2000.

Considering the poor Sanitation scenario in the rural areas, the TSC was initially launched in the State on a pilot basis in the South and West districts of the state based on the fact that bad sanitary and hygiene habits had a direct link to the health and well being of the rural populace. Later on, it was extended to the remaining two districts also. The Sanitation Campaign launched by the Ministry of Rural Development, Government of India, in the State of Sikkim has been very beneficial on the health status of the villagers where introduced.

The State Government had taken a policy decision to make Sikkim a Nirmal State (Clean State). Taking this view in mind, the Panchayati Raj Act has also been amended making it mandatory for the PRI members to construct toilet of their own in their households. In order to attain "Nirmal Gram" the State Government had taken up 10 constituencies covering 58 Gram Panchayat Units (GPUs) and 308 wards in four districts in the year 2005-06. Out of which 27 GPUs have already achieved Nirmal Gram Awards. Among them Gram Panchayat Unit number 24 Namcheybong of Pakyong Block in East Sikkim and 31 Assangthang Gram Panchayat Unit of Namchi Block in South Sikkim are also the Nirmal Gram Puraskar Awardees.

Objectives

Improving the Health status of the Society is one of the major thrust areas of the social development programmes of any country. The present study analyzes the performance of TSC and its impact on reduction in out-breaks of diseases, changes in life styles of villagers, in these NGP awarded GPUs of East and South Sikkim. Thus the major objectives of this Case Study on NGP awardees are as follows:

1. To study the current situation and practices of the people of Nirmal Gram villages about hygiene and sanitation since the implementation of TSC in the study villages.
2. To view the community's perception related to hygiene and sanitation, diseases and their reduced incidences after the intervention of TSC.
3. To analyze the extent and direction of reduction in the out-break of diseases and the overall impact of TSC on Environment, health status and life styles of the local populations.

Study Area and Sample Villages

The two ideal Village Panchayats of East and South District belonging to Pakyong and Namchi Blocks were selected as study area. In each of these blocks, two village Panchayats were selected after consulting the district level officials. These two villages of East and South district, viz. 24 Namcheybong and 31 Assangthang were reported to have attained the status of 100 per cent open defecation free Gram Panchayat Units.

With six revenue wards, 24 Namcheybong GPU falls under the jurisdiction of the Pakyong Block in East Sikkim. The GPU has a total population of 4,431 having 839 numbers of households. Out of total population 2,155 are men and 2,036 women with most of them belonging to backward class. The GPU also has a rich agricultural base providing employment to rural population. Namcheybong GPU lies across the bank of Hellkhola which is a perennial river flowing through the district. Almost 90 per cent of them are literate. The Gram Panchayat has 6 wards, namely *Kyongsee, Basnet Gaon, Ghataney Katleytar, Upper Rai Gaon, Lower Rai Gaon and Nimtar* with 423 BPL and 419 APL households. This is a fast developing village especially in community infrastructure. The Panchayat has two primary schools and one high school having a total of 897 students. Also, there is primary health sub-centre, panchayat office, post office, banks etc. Namcheybong Panchayat has witnessed many development interventions both Governmental and Non-Governmental as well as individual efforts which need to be underlined that have made this Panchayat a model not only for the district but also for the entire State because of its pioneering efforts in the field of sanitation, drinking water availability and assets maintenance, Self Help Groups movement, community participation in development projects, rain water harvesting, greening up activities and efforts in the field of education and health.

Administratively 31 Assangthang GPU is under the jurisdiction of Namchi Block of south district. 31 Assangthang GPU is comparatively a small village with a population of 1476 as per the 1991 census having 287 households. Out of the total households, 217 households belong to the BPL and 94 households belong to APL family. Assangthang GPU with a geographical area of 228.25 hectares has no perennial river flowing through the GPU. Assangthang has various spring sources, the major being Shyampani which is almost perennial in its nature. The other spring sources are like Kalsingh Dhara, Ahley Dhara which are seasonal but satisfy the need for water of the community. People of Assangthang also tap rainwater for their kitchen garden. It covers 5 revenue wards, namely Upper Assangthang, Lower Assangthang, Sangbong Dumigaon, Sangbong Ahley and Sangbong Ravigaon. Majority of the population managed their economic activity with agriculture. It is located about 5 km, away from Namchi, District headquarters. Assangthang is one of the major emerging tourist destinations in South Sikkim. This GPU already owns a helipad.

Methodology and Data

Participatory Rural Appraisal (PRA) tools such as, social mapping, transect walk and focus group discussions were used to gather information and insights into the project. A sample of 120 primary stakeholders from each GPU were randomly selected and interviewed with the help of semi structured interview schedules and focus group discussions for understanding the health impact of TSC in the GPUs.

In the process, discussions were held with key project officials at different levels, representatives of NGOs involved, non-official functionaries and beneficiaries of the project. The project details were also collected from the District Development Officers (DDOs), Block Development Officers (BDOs), Rural Development Assistants (RDAs), and the Elected Panchayats. The study includes the collection of data from Primary health centres and medical sources for confirming the positive impacts on health and reduction in the medical expenditures to be borne by the people after the intervention of TSC programme in the NGP Village.

Secondary data relating to the project were also collected from the concerned offices. The analysis of the data focuses on seeking evidence whether the TSC intervention had an impact on health and which hygiene promotion activities appear more effective at stimulating and sustaining behavioural change. The data are qualitative in nature and conclusions cannot be generalized. The analysis is presented in the form of case studies of the two selected Gram Panchayat Units.

Findings and Programme Implications

This case study is an attempt to take a stock of the achievement in NGP awardee GPUs—number 24 Namcheybong of Pakyong block in East Sikkim and 31 Assangthang of Namchi block in South Sikkim over the last two years with respect to the success of Total Sanitation Programme and its impact on health of the people. The Namcheybong of Pakyong block achieved full coverage of sanitation by June 2006 and Assangthang Gram Panchayat of Namchi block in August 2006. The major findings are as follows:

(i) 96 per cent of the population of both villages were fully aware about the programme and its objectives.
(ii) Hundred per cent respondents were using IHHLs[1] properly.
(iii) Most of the beneficiaries had adopted single pit lined IHHL while few had setup double pit IHHL.
(iv) Nearly 90 per cent of the respondents had procured the sanitary materials from their nearby open market. This is due to the lack of rural sanitary marts in their locality.
(v) In most of the BPL cases, women were cleaning the IHHLs by using phenyl and acid. In APL houses, the western style latrines were also seen, which were cleaned by the servants. It was also noticed that a small bucket with mug were also kept inside IHHLs.
(vi) Majority of houses are having piped water supply with storage tank in both GPs. The respondents in Namcheybong GP had revealed that they have sufficient amount of water for maintenance of their IHHLs. Respondents from Assangthang revealed that they face shortage of water to some extent in winter only.
(vii) With the declaration of the organic state and banning of chemical fertilizer by government of Sikkim, rural people of the state are making best use of household garbage in preparing organic manure by adopting vermi culture and other techniques for their vegetable garden as well as for agriculture purpose in both GPs. Households were also using community dustbins for disposing the garbage which were arranged by the village panchayat.

(viii) 95 per cent of the respondents were highly satisfied with quality of IHHLs in both GPs. Degree of satisfaction was more in BPL as compared to APL households. One of the major reasons for this was that BPLfamilies received subsidy while APL families did not receive any subsidy.

(ix) There was a sign of attitudinal change amongst the villagers towards open defecation due to implementation of TSC.

(x) Since most of toilets were constructed by the villagers themselves, hence, a sense of ownership has been built up due to their involvement in the construction activities.

School Sanitation and Hygiene Education

A major objective of School Sanitation and Hygiene Education was to communicate about sanitation and hygiene education through children in the families. In this regard, significant behavioural changes towards sanitation among adult members of the families have been found. As per the findings of the Focus Group Discussions (FGDs), villagers had benefited from the messages received from their children in washing hands after defecation, boiling drinking water, cutting of nails and wearing foot wears etc. It was also found that all children were using the sanitary complexes.

The introduction of SSHE programme has had an encouraging impact on the sanitation behaviour of the students in terms of regular use of toilets and zero open urination and defecation. Regular use of dustbins for waste disposal both in the classroom and the school compound was found in both the sampled GPUs. Keeping themselves and their uniform clean was a noticeable practice witnessed during field visits. The students and teachers actively participate in the cleanliness and maintenance activities of their school compound once in a month. The students, by and large, take care of the maintenance without any external support.

The messages on environmental sanitation, personal hygiene and waste disposal are being taught by the teachers on daily basis. The children were also taught about hygienic behaviours and a group of students in the school monitor on day-to-day basis the general hygiene quotient of a child.

Separate toilets for boys and girls, drinking and hand washing facilities were found in place and sufficient numbers of school children, boys and girls were constantly using these facilities. Parents' and Teachers' Associations in Primary and Junior High schools have been formed recently in both the surveyed Panchayats. Although they have not started functioning fully, they keep meeting once in a while to discuss about the development of their school in general. A syllabus on sanitation and personal hygiene practices was included as part of the curriculum in primary and secondary schools. In both the Panchayats, school complexes have been supported with strong IEC materials like hoardings to allow children to adopt hygiene practices.

In a nutshell, we may say that TSC project has really struck a balance in generating awareness about the hygiene practices and in future it is expected to yield far better result in School Sanitation and Hygiene Education.

Community Sanitary Complexes (CSCs)

Two CSCs were assisted under TSC in the Namcheybong GPU. These CSCs are exclusively constructed in those areas, where people gather in sufficient number. This is located in Nimtar ward No. 4 and Suming Milk Dairy of Namcheybong GPU. These CSCs are handed over to SHGs for operation and maintenance based on pay and use system. It is observed that the CSCs are maintained hygienically by the SHGs.

Anganwadi Sanitation

Only 2 Anganwadi centres were functioning in the Assangthang Panchayat and there is no Anganwadi centre in Namcheybong Panchayat. Both the Anganwadi Centres have been covered with baby friendly latrines in Assangthang Panchayat. All the Anganwadi centres were having sanitary latrines, which were being used by the children with the help of Anganwadi staff.

Impact of TSC on Health

Bacteria, viruses and parasites found in human waste are responsible for the transmission of water borne diseases that harm people on the large scale. The use of latrines along with the knowledge and understanding about the correlation between hygiene and diseases can minimize the transmission of water borne diseases in human beings.

Sickness Profile

Nearly one-third of both the Panchayats used to suffer from one or the other ailment before the implementation of TSC. Two third of them in both the Panchayats spend on an average Rs. 500 on their treatment during the year. Of the various ailments they suffered before the TSC programme, the pattern varied within the state. However, it emerges that many of the diseases suffered were related to unsafe water and unhygienic conditions and practices. The ailments reported may not be technically correct and many a times diarrhoea, malaria, etc. were mentioned as a general disease that many suffered, without being specific if it happened before the intervention of TSC. Three types of respondents were approached, namely women, village leaders and the health workers/doctors of PHC to examine the impact of Total Sanitation Campaign on sanitation and water borne diseases.

After the intervention of TSC, reduced incidence of disease and resultant improvement in health was observed by all three types of respondents, i.e. the women, village leaders and health workers. This report illustrates the results of the study related to the improvement in health after the TSC intervention in both Panchayats (Fig. 13.1).

In the FGD Women and Village leaders revealed that health and hygiene situation in the village was not good before 2003. The people used to suffer at the end of dry season from diarrhoea, gastroenteritis, and fever every year before introduction of TSC programme. And due to lack of awareness, the people did not give importance to these aspects. But after the TSC intervention from the past two years people revealed that more than 60 per cent of the diarrhoea cases have been reduced in Namcheybong. Nearly 50 per cent of the gastroenteritis and fever cases have been reduced in Namcheybong GPU. People also revealed that they used to have jaundice cases more in their village before TSC but now a days jaundice has been almost eliminated from their area. Details may be seen in the Figure 13.1 above.

According to the opinion of primary health worker diarrhoea and gastroenteritis seemed to be the major problem in these areas. There

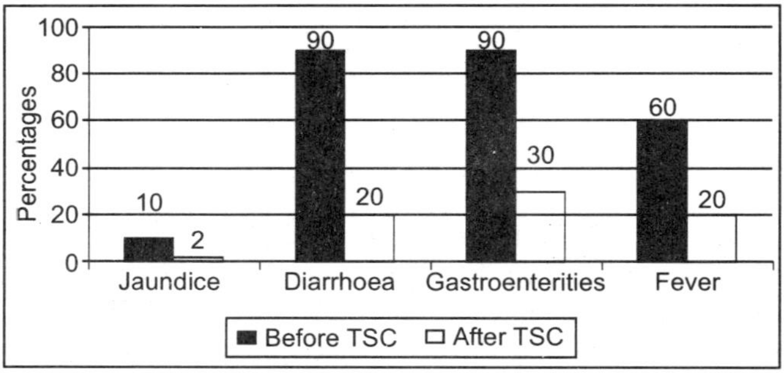

Fig. 13.1: Perception among Women and Village Leaders in Namcheybong

were approximately above 90 per cent cases of diarrhoea and gastroenteritis recorded each year which were generally caused by poor water and sanitation practices. But after the TSC intervention even these kind of common ailments are showing a sign of decline. These diseases have been reduced by improving access to clean water supplies and sanitation. Joint pain cases have also shown a sign of decline in Namcheybong GPU after the TSC intervention.

According to the women and village leaders of Assangthang Panchayat, prior to the implementation of TSC, villagers especially children used to suffer from diarrhoea. In their recollection of the memories prior to TSC, around 60 per cent of the villagers used to suffer from diarrhoea cases. In addition, diseases like fever, jaundice and even malaria were widespread. But as a result of improved sanitation in the villages because of TSC, not a single case of malaria has been found in this village in the past one year. Details may be seen in Fig. 13.2. The overall health condition of children has also improved. Now most of the people were aware and conscious of the benefit of sanitation in the village. The impact of TSC has been found significant in the sampled villages. Fear of dreaded diseases like cholera, dysentery and typhoid has been wiped out among the rural communities now.

According to the opinion of primary health worker in the sampled Panchayat water borne diseases like diarrhoea and gastroenteritis were the major ailments in the village prior to implementation of the TSC. There has been a clear decline in the number of persons affected by

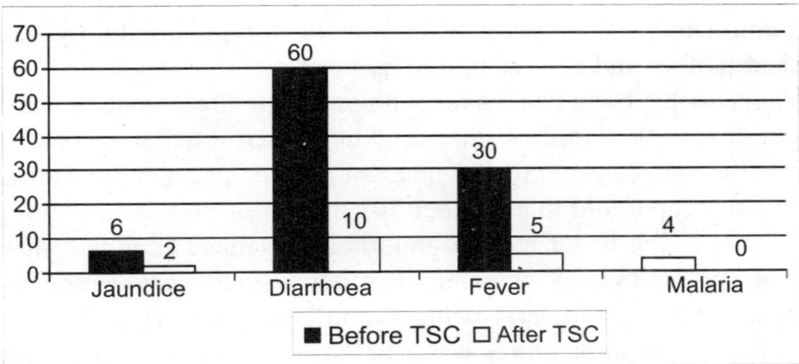

Fig. 13.2: Perception among Women and Village Leaders of Assangthang

diarrhoea and dysentery and even tuberculosis. Only one case of tuberculosis has been reported as compared to 5 in 2003. It is recorded that currently cases of sickness and subsequent wage loss were negligible. Consequently, the villagers' number of visits to PHCs had declined.

The Village leaders of both the Panchyats informed that during the study year 2006-07; no family in these villages has been badly affected by any dreaded disease. They have understood the usefulness of TSC themselves. Now they have even communicated their views on TSC to the people of nearby villages also which is a good sign of improvement.

According to the findings of the study, intervention of TSC has reduced diarrhoea and other water-related problems such as jaundice in these areas. As a result, "monthly medical costs for common illnesses have decreased in rural areas. Loss of work and loss of study days for children in the schools due to sickness have also reduced". Thus, income of households increased through savings accumulation and overall economic condition of the rural people has improved. As mentioned above, reduced incidence of diseases in these areas clearly compliments the fact that there is an improvement in awareness on sanitation and hygiene among the rural people.

With respect to the personal hygiene practices respondents of both the Panchayats revealed that almost all have started following the practice of washing hands with a soap or liquid soap after defecation and before eating; using foot wear; regular bath, wearing washed clothes and following oral hygiene.

In Namcheybong Panchayat, with respect to the storage of water, 40 per cent of the families store drinking water in tanks (cemented) which is a practice generally found among upper class people. During FGD, the people told that another 50 per cent of population prefers to store drinking water in wide-mouthed containers (drums, syntax etc.) because of ease in accessing the water. Usually narrow mouthed containers are used to carry water from distance and 10 per cent of the village population stores water in these vessels. The percentage of people who store water in the cemented tanks are little higher in Assangthang Panchayat at around 51 per cent. This is primarily because Assangthang do not have many perennial sources; hence people like to store water in large quantity to avoid the scarcity. Around 39 per cent of the village population stores water in wide-mouth containers like (Plastic tank, Drums) etc. and in Namcheybong, majority of the population stores water in narrow-mouth containers. The practice of cleaning and covering the vessels used for water storage is linked with health.

In the sample Panchayats, 100 per cent women and village leaders attributed reduction in the incidence of the above mentioned diseases because of the availability of safe water and improved sanitation practices and 100 per cent coverage in IHHL and CSL[2] so that no one defecates in open in the village.

Factors that Contributed to the Success

The credit goes to the community especially school children, teachers, Panchayats, NGOs and project officials whose synergistic efforts made the achievements possible. The factors that contributed for the success are as follows:

Decentralised Governance

Having accepted and adopted the principles and practices of democratic decentralization mainly through the Panchayats, there is greater role and participation of the Panchayats in TSC. Decentralization has ensured equitable flow of funds to all the regions of Sikkim. Decentralized planning has improved local capacity in understanding challenges related to development and in identifying strategies and programmes to meet them. It has succeeded in improving the understanding of elected representatives on a wide range of development issues and has enhanced their capability to relate them with their local situation. It has enhanced the participation of people as well as resource persons from different spheres of life in the process of local level planning. It has made local governance more responsive and transparent.

Active Role of Panchayati Raj Institutions (PRIs)

Active role of Gram Panchayat Members in both the Namcheybong and Assangthang Panchayats was noticed. Their role as a facilitator in implementation of TSC has really encouraged the villagers to take up the IHHLs, CSCs and SSHE. The Panchayat president is the main motivator for the construction of the IHHL at the village Panchayat level. Village Panchayat has also contributed for operation and maintenance of community sanitary complexes (CSCs).

Village Water and Sanitation Committees (VWSCs)

Both the village panchayats are having VWSCs, which are also Vigilance and Monitoring Committee of the Panchayats. The Panchayat President is the executive authority to implement IHHLs. He/she is also the president of VWSC. It comprises five to six members from village panchayat wards (elected); one member from local NGO representative; one woman member from a SHG group; one member from a youth club; and one member (woman) from a primary school. Their active vigilance about the schemes all the time has helped in operation, maintenance and sustainability.

Non-Governmental Organization (NGO)

Active Participation of NGOs, SHGs and CBOs of their respective Panchayats for implementation of IEC has really helped in achieving the success. As part of IEC, NGOs had conducted intensive rallies, puppet shows, posters, door-to-door campaigns and demonstrations on personal hygiene practices and the awareness programmes for the school teachers and pupils, Anganwadi workers and children.

Temples and Churches

The temples and churches have also played important role in promoting hygiene practices and environmental sanitation in the sample Panchayats. The villagers mentioned that drinking boiled water; taking daily bath; wearing washed clothes; wearing foot wear; washing hands before eating; washing hands after using toilets; and cleaning of surroundings were also preached in the temple and the church congregations.

Cohesion in the Village Community

In both the sample GPUs, we could see the clear cohesion of the village community. There were no difference found within the community with respect to caste, creed and sex. All have stood up for the general welfare of their village. Thus, this has also greatly influenced and contributed to the success of TSC in their area.

Support from the Government

The prompt funding support from the Government of India and the State Government to the district projects and subsequent recruitment of committed and hardworking team with quality training and proper orientation inputs were the steps that laid the foundation for such achievements. This helped in building a strong and informed team with well defined roles and responsibility. The vision of making Sikkim a "SWASTHYA RAJYA", by the Government of Sikkim itself signifies about the seriousness and commitment of the State Government.

IEC Programme

The IEC campaigns virtually helped the entire community to gain awareness about the health and personal hygiene issues. The extensive and creative use of IEC activities such as hoardings, songs, wall painting, flip charts, etc. made the social mobilization drive more interesting and helped in establishing a dialogue with community, which further led to behavioural change and community empowerment. Trainings, workshop and mass awareness programmes for the various stakeholders and Panchayat representatives on TSC at different levels conducted by State Institute of Rural Development, Sikkim has really moved the project one step ahead. This resulted in demand generation for establishing sanitation facilities in households, anganwadis and schools.

Attempts have been made to create mass awareness through IEC activities in schools. Competitions on various aspects like song, debate, sit and draw, drama etc. on TSC themes among the school students were also organized. Door to door publicity by the block level workers, SHG motivators, members of NGOs, social workers and others were given special emphasis. Audio cassettes on TSC in Nepali were distributed all over the state. The uniqueness about the strategy adopted under this programme was to make the programme community led and "People centred" along with involvement of political institutions, government officials, grassroots level workers, PRIs and educational institutions etc. During the campaign on sanitation, other related issues like health, hygiene, woman empowerment etc. were also emphasised upon.

Conclusion

There is a need to continue this programme and revisit some of the awarded Gram Panchayats to learn the triggers and mechanisms employed to sustain the change. Thus, it is clear that with the present level of physical achievement, the rate of growth of access to sanitation facilities has really improved the health status of these studied Panchayats. The Innovative components of this project in these Panchayats would help in replicating the project in other uncovered problem villages/districts within and outside the state. Hygiene education should be promoted on a wider scale. Inter-school competitions on debate, poetry and essay should be conducted on topics like sanitation and personal hygiene. The people across the villages have shown keen interest in the usages of constructed latrines. There has been appreciable rise in personal, domestic and village cleanliness as well as overall environment standards. Hence people should be encouraged to share their experiences with other villages.

NOTES

1. IHHL—Individual household latrine.
2. CSL—Community sanitary latrine.

Index